A Librarian's Guide to the Internet

CHANDOS
INFORMATION PROFESSIONAL SERIES

Chandos' new series of books are aimed at the busy information professional. They have been specially commissioned to provide the reader with an authoritative view of current thinking. They are designed to provide easy-to-read and (most importantly) practical coverage of topics that are of interest to librarians and other information professionals. If you would like a full listing of current and forthcoming titles, please visit our web site **www.library-chandospublishing.com** or contact Hannah Grace-Williams on email info@chandospublishing.com or telephone number +44 (0) 1865 884447.

New authors: we are always pleased to receive ideas for new titles; if you would like to write a book for Chandos, please contact Dr Glyn Jones on email gjones@chandospublishing.com or telephone number +44 (0) 1865 884447.

Bulk orders: some organisations buy a number of copies of our books. If you are interested in doing this, we would be pleased to discuss a discount. Please contact Hannah Grace-Williams on email info@chandospublishing.com or telephone number +44 (0) 1865 884447.

A Librarian's Guide to the Internet

Searching and evaluating information

JEANNE FROIDEVAUX MÜLLER

Chandos Publishing

Oxford · England · New Hampshire · USA

Chandos Publishing (Oxford) Limited
Chandos House
5 & 6 Steadys Lane
Stanton Harcourt
Oxford OX29 5RL
UK
Tel: +44 (0) 1865 884447 Fax: +44 (0) 1865 884448
Email: info@chandospublishing.com
www.library-chandospublishing.com

Chandos Publishing USA
3 Front Street, Suite 331
PO Box 338
Rollinsford, NH 03869
USA
Tel: 603 749 9171 Fax: 603 749 6155
Email: BizBks@aol.com

First published in Great Britain in 2003

ISBN:
1 84334 055 0 (paperback)
1 84334 056 9 (hardback)

© J.F. Müller, 2003

British Library Cataloguing-in-Publication Data.
A catalogue record for this book is available from the British Library.

Typeset by Monolith – www.monolith.uk.com
Printed in the UK and USA

To Iwan

Contents

Acknowledgements

For their contributions, ideas and insights into our profession, I would like to thank:

- Roddy MacLeod, Senior Subject Librarian, Heriot-Watt University, Edinburgh;

- Randy Metcalfe, Communications Manager, Humbul Humanities Hub, Oxford University, Oxford;

- Judith Howells, Assistant Professional Adviser, Chartered Institute of Library and Information Professionals (CILIP), London.

My thanks also go to:

- the head of the public library of Thun, Mrs Else Bäumlin, who let me write parts of this book during office hours;

- Graham Coult, editor of *Managing Information*, who started all this by asking questions in the online forum of that publication;

- Dr Glyn Jones, my publisher, at Chandos Publishing in Oxford.

I would also like to thank Google for their permission to use parts of the text and images of their website.

About the author

Jeanne Froidevaux Müller is a frequent contributor to and author of a regular column in the respected magazine *Managing Information*, and is currently based at the public library in the city of Thun, Switzerland, where she is responsible for the library system and statistics, as well as being head of cataloguing.

Following a banking apprenticeship in Bern, Switzerland, the country of her birth, she attended the English Language School in Poole, Dorset and gained the Cambridge Proficiency Certificate.

In 1988 she took a position with the Swiss Cancer League as secretary to the Executive Director and went on to undertake a postgraduate diploma course on Information and Documentation at the College of Engineering in Chur between 1994 and 1996.

During this time the author began work on building a documentation service at the Cancer League, the only public library in Europe devoted to literature on cancer for patients, and was head of the library from 1999 to October 2002. She was also responsible for the design and implementation of the Cancer League's first website in 1992, and for recruiting and supervising the web publisher.

The author may be contacted via the publishers.

Introduction

Of all the needs a book has the chief need is that it be readable.
Anthony Trollope

Scores of books about efficient search strategies have been written and will, doubtless, be written again. I would like to offer you guidance on this subject that you can use on a daily basis – to offer you a handy and practical working tool. This book is intended for librarians and other information professionals who have very little experience of working with the Internet. Of course I hope that there will be a few tips and hints that even experienced users – or indeed any person who reads this book – may find helpful.

While researching for this book I realised how little we really know and how vast is the amount of information available. On occasions I have found it difficult not to get lost in the subject I have been researching, often chancing upon a completely different topic and having to concentrate hard not to become distracted. In Chapters 6 and 7, I offer a selection of web resources that might prove useful in your daily work. The lists are by no means exhaustive but I would like to think they give a good foundation and you are encouraged to develop your own list of resources as you go along.

It is not as if we are responsible for the content of a website. The World Wide Web is a tool to be used to our advantage, not something to be afraid of. The information found on the Web is never the responsibility of the web itself, which is simply a huge collection of thousands of different sources. Just because one source is of bad quality does not mean that all the other sources are bad as well. This is something very important and I think we have to remind ourselves from time to time of the fact.

Because of the rapid changes in this field, experience does not count in the same sense as it used to. It used to be possible to say 'I learned this 15 years ago, the knowledge is still the same and therefore I am a pro'. Sadly – or perhaps not – this is not the case anymore. In our fast changing world, it is vital that we adapt ourselves constantly and change with the times. As librarians, we know all about books, libraries and the book trade. We know library classification systems and we have an understanding of education and culture. Usually, we also have one or several subjects that we are particularly knowledgeable in, e.g. English literature or gardening. But we should not forget that the Internet is just a tool – nothing more, nothing less – to obtain information. We are knowledgeable in our profession and we should use the Internet as a professional working tool.

I take it that you know how to get connected to the Internet, how to participate in newsgroups and communicate via e-mail. I take it that you have some experience and that perhaps you do not want to read the 'Dummies guide to the Internet'. I would like to offer you a usable, realistic guide that you, hopefully, can use in your daily work. I would like to guide you through the maze of information available on the Internet. I would like to teach you enough of my knowledge that you gain the familiarity and confidence usually only to be gained while working on a day-to-day basis with a subject.

I think there is a friendly coexistence between books, libraries and the Internet and that people who read and who are used to using libraries (and I hope this includes librarians!) will find it easier to use and navigate the Web. Readers are familiar with the virtual worlds that books and stories create. Library users know of the pleasure of entering a library and, while knowing and acknowledging perfectly well how the library books are catalogued and put in a special order, getting lost on the way and finding new things, new stories, new subjects ... I think this is what makes the use of a library so special. Avid and regular readers are used to processing words and information; they know what to do with words. I have more than once seen young people – not very avid readers – overwhelmed by a screen full of words, whereas I have also watched many older people – regular readers – having no problem whatsoever in finding and using information from the Internet.

One example that struck me as particularly typical was someone who said that they did not like computers – they had never handled a typewriter, let alone a computer, and basically didn't know the front from the back. But once they realised they could get information they were very interested in (in this case opera programmes from Paris) and it was much easier than the method they were used to, they were absolutely hooked. This person also had absolutely no problems whatsoever booking online tickets for the opera, whereas I have seen other, much younger people who cannot be bothered to use a credit card or to read the instructions on how to book.

As Nigella Lawson in her brilliant book *How to Eat* so aptly put it: 'As much as possible, I have wanted to make you feel that I am there with you, in your kitchen, as you cook. The book that follows is the conversation we might be having.'[1] And I sincerely hope that you will find that this book, which has given me immense joy to write, will fulfil its aim and be the readable companion it is intended.

Note on Internet addresses

I will use Internet addresses, the so-called URL, or unique resource locator, throughout the text. In order to make the reading of the text easier, Internet addresses are given in italic and without the Internet standard of blue font type or underlining.

All Internet addresses used will also be listed at the end of the book in alphabetical order. All Internet addresses were checked between January and April 2003 and were correct at that time.

Microsoft Internet Explorer is at the time of writing the market leader; therefore, I use this browser in my examples. But as I said before, I would like to enable you to concentrate on the content, and not too much on the tools used to obtain the necessary information.

Note

1. Nigella Lawson (1999) *How to Eat: The Pleasures and Principles of Good Food.* London: Chatto & Windus.

From data to the Internet

Knowledge comes, but wisdom lingers.

Alfred, Lord Tennyson

Sometimes I get the feeling that I have had enough of the Internet and the World Wide Web, that everyone around me is talking about nothing else, often knowing little about it. All the magazines and all the newspapers are full of it. It's only human nature that when we think we know all about something, we stop paying attention to it. This is a dangerous attitude because it makes us complacent, perhaps even sloppy.

Very often, some of the words that we hear and use every day, and which for many of us come from, if not quite a closed book, perhaps a book written in a not entirely mastered foreign language. I have written this book using non-technical terms as far as possible, and where technical issues cannot be avoided I have tried to explain them with non-technical comparisons. The following list is by no means exhaustive and other technical expressions will be explained throughout the book.

- *The Internet* has been called many things. One of them is: a network of networks linking computers to computers. Computers communicate together using something called TCP/IP. TCP means Transmission Control Protocol; IP stands for Internet Protocol. Each computer runs software to provide information and/or to access and view information. The Internet is like a transport vehicle for the information stored in files or documents on another computer. It is, however, very important to remember that the Internet itself does not contain information. It is therefore not quite correct to say a 'document was found on the Internet'. It would be more correct to say it was found *through* or *using* the Internet.

Computers on the Internet may use one or all of the following Internet services:

- *Electronic mail* or e-mail. Permits you to send and receive mail.

- *The World Wide Web (WWW or 'the Web')*. The Web incorporates all of the Internet services above and much more. It is the part of the Internet that allows users to retrieve documents, view images, animation and video, listen to sound files, speak and hear voice messages, and view programmes. When you log onto the Internet using a browser, usually Microsoft's Internet Explorer, you are viewing documents on the Web. The current foundation on which the Web functions is the programming language called HTML, short for hypertext markup language.

- *HTML*. Hypertext is the ability to add links to web pages. Links are areas in a page or buttons or graphics on which you can click your mouse to retrieve another document into your computer. This 'clickability' using hypertext links is the feature which is unique and revolutionary about the Web.

- *Browser*. A browser is a computer program that enables you to use the computer to view documents on the Web. It enables you to access the Internet taking advantage of text formatting, hypertext links, images, sounds, motion and other features. Currently, Internet Explorer is the leading 'graphical browser' in the world.

However, when all is said and done, the Internet is simply a means to distribute and to gather information which can then, hopefully, be transformed into knowledge.

Today, it is simply impossible for an individual to transform all available information regarding a particular problem into knowledge. In most cases, a lifetime would not be enough to absorb what is available and the gap between what is available and its usage gets bigger every day. At the same time, search and data storage technologies are being advanced in similar fashion. However, the capacity of the human brain for information processing remains limited. Someone once calculated that between 95 per cent and 99 per cent of the information produced daily inevitably remains unused.

Let us now have a look at the differences between data, information and knowledge.

Data:

- are isolated facts and figures used to describe reality but which have not been interpreted;
- can be factual information, e.g. measurements or statistics, used as a basis for reasoning, discussion or calculation;
- means any numbers or any characters that a computer can use.

Information:

- is data given a meaning by way of relational connection;
- is data that is processed to be useful (or not);
- only becomes knowledge when it is individually processed and if there is a reference, a relation to one's own experience;
- is obtained from investigation, study or instruction;
- is facts or data, especially pertaining to a particular subject or regarded as significant;
- can mean news or a signal or sequence of symbols, e.g. in a radio transmission or computing;
- can mean the communication or reception of facts or ideas;
- provides answers to 'who?', 'what?', 'where?' and 'when?' questions.

Knowledge:

- is information, understanding or skills acquired through learning or experience;
- is the total body of known facts, or those associated with a particular subject;
- in philosophy is a justified or verifiable belief, as distinct from opinion;
- describes the awareness of something and is always bound to people;
- is the application of data and information;
- answers 'how?' questions.

After knowledge, the human mind is also capable of understanding and wisdom. Understanding may be defined as the appreciation of why things are and wisdom as evaluated understanding.

It has been rather fashionable over the last few years – no doubt sparked by the growth of the Web and the ensuing information overkill – to connect all this talk about data and knowledge solely to the use of the Internet. True as this may be, it is no more or less true regarding the Web as it is for conventional media. But of course, data, information and human knowledge and what we make of it has been around since before the Web was created. Unfortunately (or fortunately?), the reading of books does not make one automatically wise and clever. Nor does the reading of pages found on the Web make us knowledgeable. Information, no matter where it is found, does not automatically transform itself miraculously into knowledge and wisdom in the head of the reader. The German physicist Georg Christoph Lichtenberg (1742–99) said: 'Wenn ein Kopf und ein Buch zusammenstossen und es klingt hohl, ist das nicht allemal das Buch [When a head and a book collide and it sounds hollow, it is not always the book].'

3

Search strategies

Strategy and tactics do not change. Only the means of applying them are different.

General Patton

Tried, tested and trusted personal search strategies

The word information has become a much cited catchword. It releases a myriad of associations in most people. Whether we like it or not, we are today in an age of rapid changes where the amount of information – useful and useless – expands in a way which is sometimes hard to understand. To be able to keep abreast of the big picture in this environment gets more difficult every day. To be able to generate knowledge out of this information sometimes seems to be almost impossible and the World Wide Web – which, seemingly, offers a wealth of information on every imaginable subject under the sun at the touch of a button – furthers this information overload. Every paper, newspaper article and book will tell you that there is no way for anyone to search the entire Web, and any search tool claiming to offer it all to you is simply not telling the truth. Your strategy should therefore be to get the most and best out of the Web in the most efficient way and with the least effort involved.

One of the most important tools for successfully searching for information is professional curiosity. Let us slip into the role of a reader here. On entering a library for the first time, some patience is in order. No library lets itself be accessed on the first visit, and no library opens itself up completely to a visitor, not even after many years and visits. But library users know this. This is what makes a library so fascinating for them – knowing there is an almost limitless amount of information to be found on the library shelves. Readers, I think, have an advantage over many others in using the Internet. To roam in virtual worlds – is this not what reading is all about? Readers are quite aware of the alleged dangers that lurk in these virtual worlds. Readers know of confusions of appearance and reality, of isolation, of loneliness and loss of identity, of the addiction of always wanting more and more of the stuff that virtual worlds are made of. Those well-meaning and moralising critics who claimed to know better warned readers of these dangers 200 years ago. Then it was the novel that was so dangerous.

It seems to me that readers of books are also at an advantage because they have had many years of experience in dealing with words and text. The reader is like a pedestrian, as opposed to the web surfer. The reader knows when it is necessary to change his or her reading speed, from striding to strolling or even sauntering. They are used to making time for notes, to pause for a thought, to reread a particularly well-written sentence. They can make notes of the ways they used to get somewhere and they can, if they so choose, go back to them. On the other hand, the surfer is not able to find the places again that they passed on their way through water and waves. They do not have time to look around. They dance on the crest of a wave and make sure they get on. Were they to pause, they would surely drown.

Avid readers are and always have been quite capable of mastering vast amounts of information. Imagine how much information every buyer of a newspaper is confronted with on entering a newsagent, and how easily they can put all the unwanted information aside by simply choosing to ignore it. Information is always like a tidal wave and those who are unable to orient themselves will be drowned. This is true with every daily newspaper, with every book in every library, but it is also true with the Web.

The following search tips and hints are based on almost eight years' experience. Some of them may sound banal, but in the end that is what it is all about: find methods and search strategies that work for you and for the way you work. It needs experience to develop your own tricks and knacks and secret systems. There is no 'best' strategy as such. Often, the success of a search depends on the subject you are researching: if you are searching for information on computers you will use the Web differently than if you are searching for material on, say, domestic politics. The sources are completely different. I will, in this chapter, demonstrate my personal search strategies, developed over the years. They are certainly not complete nor are they infallible, but they have helped me in my job. Those search methods and strategies I have developed over the years are as follows:

Search method 1: What do I want to know?

Search method 2: Do I know my subject?

Search method 3: If you do not know your subject, search for a good source first

Search method 4: Talk to others

Search method 5: Ask other people

Search method 6: Have a look at what others search for

Search method 7: Search for information directly

Search method 8: Be specific

Search method 1: What do I want to know?

What are you really searching? In searching the Web, we are, as often as not, guessing what subject headings or words will be in the pages we want to find.

Try to formulate your search words in your head or on paper. This helps to concentrate your thoughts. Try to think of alternative words. One of my scribbled search strategies looks like this:

Example: searching for facts on coffee plantations and coffee growing

Coffee = too common a word, don't use

Coffee plantation
Coffee farm
Coffee tree
Coffee plant

Latin name?

Do I know any sources, names? = Max Havelaar, Starbucks

Here, of course, a librarian has an advantage over the average user because we are used to thesauri and thinking of alternative descriptions and words.

Search method 2: Do I know my subject?

Whether you know the subject you are researching or not has a direct influence on your search strategy. You are more likely to know where to start searching if you know what you are looking for. You will probably already know some of the major Internet resources in your field. Perhaps you are responsible for a particular subject in your library. For example, let us assume you are responsible for the Arts section (Dewey 700). You will no doubt read the relevant magazines, reviews, newspaper articles and books. They all list relevant websites. Make a note of them and perhaps, on a weekly basis, check them out. Get to know the sites on your subject. This, again, will give you an advantage over the average user.

Search method 3: If you do not know your subject, search for a good source first

Do not search for the information itself first. Search for an appropriate source that might have the information you are looking for. This is a fast method with good results. It is also the most 'natural' method, but it tends to be forgotten, because the temptations to search directly with the search engines is too great. This method is also useful if you don't yet quite know what exactly it is you are looking for – which happens more often than you might think. If you have to write a report on a particular subject, you know the broad outline, but how you want to put it into action is not yet quite clear. For this you need to know what interesting information is available on your subject.

The method discussed here usually gets quick results, but needs some experience in searching techniques. The basic idea is as follows: it should be easier to find information in a place where it has already been collected, filed, classified and perhaps even evaluated. If you are looking for a phone number, it is only natural that you look the number up in a phone directory, because that is where phone numbers are stored – you know this from experience. The Internet gives you access to many such sources on various subjects.

Some of these sources were only made known to a larger public thanks to the Internet and some existed long before the Internet boom. Only the means of obtaining them was different: perhaps you had to make a phone call, perhaps you had to write a letter or go somewhere in person. The Internet has made much of this easier, though the basic procedure stays the same. If you are looking for a phone number, you don't just start shouting in the streets, ask the next person you happen to meet or look for it at the petrol station. You take the phone book and look the number up.

With the Internet it is the same. The only difference is that we have to learn where these information sources are located. We already know many sources on the Internet; others we have yet to find. Remember: the Internet is only a means of communication – nothing more and nothing less.

This approach is also important regarding the evaluation of websites: if you get information from a source that you know and trust, you may assume the same is true if this source is now online. The phone numbers that are published on the Web through a telephone company are hardly less reliable than the printed ones. On the contrary, they are probably more current. Whoever seeks reliable information on the Web has to search for reliable sources first – sources that are perhaps already known to him or her.

The search for good sources is based on two simple questions:

Who might offer the information I am looking for?

Try to think of who might have an interest in publishing it. The answer is – an institution. This can be a certain authority, a newspaper archive or a museum, but it can also be a company or a professional database host. Usually there are several alternatives. If you are searching for a certain product, a good source may therefore be the company that manufactures this product. On the other hand, organisations or companies that deal in such products or have an interest in them might also be a good source. This can, for example, be a professional magazine, a consumer organisation or a market research company. Newspaper archives can also be good sources: many newspapers and magazines offer online editions, most of them with archives in databases. However, while a few years ago most newspaper online versions, including their archives, were free of charge, many of them have changed to a system where it is necessary to register and pay a certain fee.

How do I get to this information?

The answer to this can of course be that the chosen source is not available on the Internet. The chances for success vary from one line of business to another. Experienced Internet users will have developed an instinct for what kind of information can be found within a reasonable timeframe. To discover the limits/limitations of the Internet, the best way is to test them.

Certain subjects are better represented than others and are therefore easier to search for than others. These subjects are traditionally: computer and telecommunications, technical and scientific information, sex, hobbies and 'fringe groups'. Subjects that are of particular interest to the US population and its economy are still better covered than European or Asian ones, but this is also changing.

This short example is by no means complete – it is simply meant to stimulate your imagination. The fact that it is so easy to get information on the Web also multiplies the amount of sources that can be tapped into to get that information. Therefore, the more thought you put into the selection of your sources and the question 'who might publish this information?', the easier your search will be.

Search method 4: Talk to others

Talk to your colleagues. Swap techniques and experiences with them. Perhaps the person working in another department of your library has been using an Internet resource for months, and you have been looking in vain for it for months...

Search method 5: Ask other people

This strategy is almost banal in its efficiency. Let others do the work for you. There are many Internet users out there who are experienced specialists, willing to share their knowledge in professional foras and newsgroups. Use this strategy if you have already tried some other methods that did not yield any results.

But there are also drawbacks to this method: it can be slow and unreliable. It will depend on whether other users will answer your questions correctly and within a useful period of time. Both these factors are impossible to foretell accurately. However, for searches over a longer period of time, this strategy may lead you to interesting sources and information.

For certain questions it might be useful to look to newsgroups and the Usenet for information. A good web-based directory to assist in locating e-mail discussion groups and Usenet newsgroups is Liszt.[1] It contains thousands of newsletters and discussion groups.

The Usenet is a collection of user-submitted notes or messages on various subjects that are posted to servers on a worldwide network. Each subject collection of posted notes is known as a newsgroup. There are thousands of newsgroups and it is possible for you to form a new one. On the Web, Google and other sites provide a subject-oriented directory as well as a search approach to newsgroups, and help you register to participate in them.

A newsgroup, then, is a discussion forum about a particular subject consisting of messages written to a central Internet site and redistributed through Usenet, a worldwide network of news discussion groups. Usenet as we know it today has grown to thousands of newsgroups and discussion lists, hosted all over the world and covering every conceivable topic about which humans feel the need to talk.

In 1995, efforts were made to provide a user-friendly interface to the original Usenet. Newsgroups are now organised into subject hierarchies, with the first few letters of the newsgroup name indicating the major subject category and subcategories represented by a subtopic name. Many subjects have multiple levels of subtopics. Some major subject categories are: news, rec (recreation), soc (society), sci (science) and comp (computers).

Users can post to existing newsgroups, respond to previous posts and create new newsgroups. Newcomers to newsgroups are requested to learn basic Usenet netiquette and to get familiar with a newsgroup before posting to it. It is also possible to subscribe to the postings on a particular newsgroup. Some newsgroups are moderated by a designated person who decides which postings to allow or to remove; however, most newsgroups are not moderated.

To come back to our example of Google: Google offers a way to post messages on Usenet through Google Groups.

Usenet is like a tree with many branches and twigs. The main branches lead to the top-level discussion categories (such as 'alt' – see below). Follow one of the branches and you will find small twigs (such as alt.animals), which lead to even smaller twigs containing messages divided into even more specific topics (such as alt.animals.dogs). Ultimately, your journey will take you to the smallest part of the data stream – the part containing messages from people who are interested in one particular topic (such as alt.animals.dogs.beagles).

The different parts of a newsgroup's name are always separated by a full point, a traditional categorisation symbol in the computer world. Each newsgroup contains threads made up of messages (also referred to as 'articles' or 'postings') that look like e-mail between one user and another, but can be read by anyone accessing that particular newsgroup.

The main groups, as listed in Google, are:

- **alt.** (alternative) – any conceivable topic;
- **biz.** (business) – business products, services, reviews;
- **comp.** (computers) – hardware, software, consumer information;
- **humanities.** (humanities) – fine art, literature, philosophy;
- **misc.** (miscellaneous) – employment, health and much more;
- **news.** (news) – information about Usenet news;
- **rec.** (recreation) – games, hobbies, sports;
- **talk.** (talk) – current issues and debates;
- **sci.** (science) – applied science, social science;
- **soc.** (society) – social issues, culture.

This all sounds very easy and sometimes it can be the last resort for a question that has remained unanswered through all other search possibilities.

A word of caution is perhaps needed while dealing with newsgroups (especially unmoderated ones). Personally, I hardly ever use the services of newsgroups. But whether you decide to use them or not is of course a decision you have to make for yourself. Even if you decide not to use them, it is a good idea to have a look at a few of them, so that you know what they are all about and what you are missing out on. However, I am always very sceptical about newsgroups – below are a few examples of why.

The following example was taken from a literary discussion group:

Message 21 in thread
From: bobgrumman@nut-n-but.net (bobgrumman@nut-n-but.net)
Subject: Re: Was Albert Einstein a hoax?
View this article only
Newsgroups: humanities.lit.authors.shakespeare
Date: 2003-02-08 17:51:14 PST

'Neil Brennen' <chessnewsnospam@mindspring.com> wrote:

> *I'm crossposting this so one of the premier anti-Einstein cranks on the Internet, Elizabeth Weir, can see it. Like Sam Sloan, Weir doubles as an anti-Shakespearean wack, although her claim for the 'true author' is Bacon, as opposed to Sloan's candidate, Oxford's daughter.*

> *I hope David Webb will comment as well.*

I'll comment.

Don't litter on our newsgroup, Brennen.

There is no good reason to crosspost.

I totally disagree, Greg. This newsgroup is mainly devoted to Shakespeare crankery. Hence, similar kinds of crankery are relevant. Aside from that, we've discussed Einstein cranks before at HLAS.

Conduct your conversations where they belong.
We have our own idiots and don't need other
idiots from other newsgroups. Don't pretend
we share your interests.

I doubt that he's pretending we share his interests. I think he is posting material he thinks and hopes may interest us, as it did me. Moreover, I think the more idiots we get here, the better. The current ones are getting boring.

I don't understand Greg's problem with Neil, but I hope he gets over it.
– Bob G.

Not much new information on Shakespeare, is there? Even if I could find information in a discussion group that I would find nowhere else, I do not think that I could be bothered with this tone.

Let us now look at the rules that are established, but unfortunately are not used by many people. The complete netiquette can be found on Google's[2] website and it is important that we know and follow these rules:

- Never forget that the person on the other side is human.
- Don't assume that a person is speaking for their organisation.
- Be careful what you say about others.
- Be brief.
- Write well.
- Use descriptive subject lines.
- Think about your audience.
- Be careful with humour and sarcasm.
- Only post a message once.
- Use mail instead of posting a follow-up.
- Summarise what you are following up.
- Cite appropriate references.
- Mark answers or spoilers.
- Limit line length and avoid control characters.
- Do not use Usenet as an advertising medium.
- Avoid posting to multiple newsgroups.

To me, of particular importance is to remember that there is a human being on the other side of the connection and, because of that, to be very careful with humour and sarcasm. I also think it is of the utmost importance to be careful of what you say about others. When I have to write difficult e-mails or if I am not sure I have put it as well as I should, I get up from my desk, have a coffee, or open the window, and then go back to the e-mail and read it again before I send it. This has worked quite well for me.

A good example of a professional, moderated discussion group is the forum to be found on the website of *Managing Information*.[3] Their discussion board is moderated by the editor, and all illegal or offensive messages will be deleted. It also clearly states that participants are asked to comply with UK and international copyright law.

Search method 6: Have a look at what others search for

Looking at what others are searching for may be interesting, perhaps entertaining and sometimes even instructive. Metacrawler's Metaspy[4] offers filtered and unfiltered spy software. Google's Zeitgeist[5] lets you see what others are searching for. It analyses search patterns and trends on a monthly, weekly and daily basis.

Search method 7: Search for information directly

This is the method I use most often. It is also the single most widely used search method and certainly has its advantages. Search engines are used to get directly to Internet addresses of websites that contain the information you are looking for. This method is easy, simple and in many cases more than adequate. For the inexperienced researcher, this may be a fallacy, because it is easy to waste too much time and to get lost with this method. However, it is also a useful method if you are looking for something particular and are able to put this into clear and precise words. More of this search method follows in the chapter about search engines.

Another possibility of direct searching is with the Internet address. If you know the Internet address of a site you wish to visit, you can use a web browser to access that site. All you need to do is type the URL in the appropriate location window. URL stands for uniform resource locator and specifies the Internet address of the electronic document. Every file on the Internet, no matter what its access protocol, has a unique URL which web browsers use to retrieve the file from the host computer and the directory in which it resides. This file is then displayed on your monitor.

Any of these addresses can be typed into the location window of a web browser. Sometimes, even if I am not quite sure, I just type in an address that I think is correct. Usually this works with well-known companies and large institutions. For example, if you type in *http://www.shell.co.uk* because you assume that the company Shell has a site registered in England, you will notice in the location window that it changes automatically to *http:www.shell.com/home/framework?siteId=uk-en*.

Search tip: looking for scientific information

If you are searching for scientific information, it is a good idea to exclude sites with the domain .com. To do this, use the advanced search function. In Google it is under: 'Domain: Don't return results from site or domain .com'.

Search method 8: Be specific

Be as specific as you can in formulating your search. You must tell the system what you know, because no search engine and not even the best software can read your thoughts. Let the search engine know what you know! Imagine, if a library customer came up to you and asked: 'Book?' What would you do? Would you know whether your customer wanted to borrow a book, bring a book back, whether he was a bookseller, or an antiquarian interested in a particular book in your collection or ...?

Since search engines cannot read thoughts, the more information you give them the better it usually is. The more specific and clear your search is, the more likely it is you will find what you are looking for. Do not be afraid to tell a search engine exactly what you are looking for. For example, if you want information about old tea roses, search for 'old tea roses', not for 'roses'. Or even better, search for exactly what the problem is: 'How do I prune old tea roses?' for example. You will be surprised at how often this works.

Example

While cataloguing the DVD *Anna and the King* with Jodie Foster, I could not remember what Siam is called today. So I went to Google and typed in the following search question:

"used to be called Siam"

This got me, obviously, a great many pages as a result. But I only needed to look at the first three descriptions of the pages

---

to find out that Siam is now Thailand. There was no need to look at the pages themselves and it took me about 20 seconds.

Here are the first five hits:

The Siamese Cat

... if the "Royal Cat of Siam", the companion of kings and priests, and guardian of the royal palace, actually originated in Thailand (which *used to be called Siam* ...

home.earthlink.net/~jcissik/siam.htm – 8k – Cached – Similar pages

International Friends in Asia

... Korea, North, Taiwan (also called Republic of China). Korea, South, Thailand (*used to be called Siam*). Laos, Tibet (a region of China). Vietnam ...

internatlfriends.crosswinds.net/asia.htm – 8k – Cached – Similar pages

ATRA: Library: Who Made The Thailand Ridgeback Dog?

... In ancient times, the King of Vietnam was in trouble with his people. He fled to Thailand and stayed with the King of Siam (Thailand *used to be called Siam*) ...

www.thaidog.org/atra/who_made.html – 16k – Cached – Similar pages

Fun and Sharing

... They hope the eyes see where the fish are. ...that Thailand *used to be called Siam* (as it is called in the musical The King and I). ...

www.kulturekids.org/fun_sharing.htm – 23k – Cached – Similar pages

> Useless Facts – Geography
>
> ... The largest city in Africa is Cairo in Egypt. Thailand *used to be called Siam*. The Sahara desert is expanding half a mile south every year. ...
>
> *www.angelfire.com/ca6/uselessfacts/geo/004.html* – 4k – Cached – Similar pages

Sometimes, it is difficult to be specific to begin with. Occasionally I do not know what I am looking for. Perhaps it is a subject that I am unfamiliar with or I have to search for something in a language that I am not fluent in. In this situation, I use what I call the *funnel method*. Start with a broad term or an unspecific word. See what results you get. And then go on from there.

While you do a search, do not ignore interesting, but to you unknown, addresses that you chance upon. It is very important to have a look at new and unknown things on a regular basis.

One important tip – and for this you do not even need a computer – is to define which method and instruments you need for your particular search before you start searching. Of course, the aim of your endeavours is ultimately to find the information you need. The most direct route is, often, the most time-consuming one. Searching on the Internet always entails more or less big detours: the skill is to find the 'fastest detour'. This is ultimately a matter of experience – and creativity. The 'chaos' in the web is nobody's fault – try to be flexible about it! Knowledge of the content should give you the confidence to deal with it. It is in the nature of this technology that there are rapid changes, changes almost every day. It may well be that the examples given in this book will not be accurate by mid-2004, or even at the time of going to press.

You should keep this in mind. The examples I give will make it easier for me to demonstrate a point or a concept. My aim is to give you enough handy tips and strategies so that it will not matter if next year all the well-known search engines are using even better technology. You will have enough confidence and familiarity with it to be able to deal with any changes that might be made as long as you keep working with it.

Notes

1. *http://www.liszt.com*
2. *http://www.google.com/groups/posting_style.htm.*
3. *http://www.managinginformation.com*
4. *http://www.metaspy.com*
5. *http://www.google.com/press/zeitgeist.html*

Search engines, directories and gateways

Everybody gets so much information all day long that they lose their common sense.

Gertrude Stein

Basically, a search engine is a searchable database of Internet files collected by a computer program. A search engine consists of three parts: a spider, an index and a search engine mechanism.

The spider (sometimes called a crawler, a robot, a worm or a bot) is a program that traverses the Web from link to link, identifying and reading pages and then storing them in the index.

The index is a database containing a copy of each web page gathered by the spider.

The search engine mechanism is the software that enables you to query the index and that usually returns results ranked in order of relevancy. The program receives your search request, compares it to the entries in the index and returns the results to you. There are no selection criteria for the collection of files, though evaluation can be applied to the ranking of results.

Now, before you even consider using a search engine, read the search hints particular to that search engine. You may say this is too obvious, or only for the inexperienced, or that you do not have the time for it, but in my experience this is one of the most important points and one that is easily overlooked. Reading the search tips will give you an advantage over the everyday user and it will give you confidence. This in turn will make people trust you since you will know what you are talking about. Let me put this another way: do you actually know anyone who has read the search hints?

Major search engines

The following list of major search engines and the accompanying descriptions were taken from the web page of Search Engine Watch[1] in January 2003. These engines are considered to be 'major' because they are either well known or well used.

Google[2]

Twice-voted the Most Outstanding Search Engine by Search Engine Watch readers, Google has a well-deserved reputation as the top choice for those searching the Web. The crawler-based service provides both comprehensive coverage of the Web along with great relevancy. It's highly recommended as a first stop in your hunt for whatever you are looking for.

Google provides the option to find more than web pages, however. Using 'tabs' on the top of the search box on the Google homepage, you can easily seek out images from across the Web, take part in discussions that are taking place on Usenet newsgroups or scan through human-compiled information provided from the Open Directory (see below).

Google is also known for the wide range of features it offers, such as cached links that let you 'resurrect' dead pages or see older versions of recently changed ones. It offers excellent spellchecking, easy access to dictionary definitions, integrated stock quotes, street maps, telephone numbers and more. The toolbar has also won popular acclaim for the easy access it provides to Google and its features directly through the Internet Explorer browser.

Google was originally a project by Stanford University students Larry Page and Sergey Brin called BackRub. By 1998, the name had been changed to Google, and the project jumped off campus and became the private company Google. It remains privately held today.

AllTheWeb.com (FAST)[3]

An excellent crawler-based search engine, All The Web provides both comprehensive coverage of the Web and outstanding relevancy. If you have tried Google and didn't find what you were looking for, All The Web should probably be next on your list. Indeed, it's a first-stop search engine for some. In addition to web page results, AllTheWeb.com provides the ability to search for news stories, pictures, video clips, MP3s and FTP files. The site is operated by FAST and used as a showcase for FAST's search technology. AllTheWeb.com/FAST results are also provided to other search sites around the world, with its strongest partnership being with Terra Lycos. AllTheWeb.com launched in May 1999.

Yahoo![4]

Launched in 1994, Yahoo! is the Web's oldest 'directory', a place where human editors organise websites into categories. However, in October 2002, Yahoo! made a giant shift to using Google's crawler-based listings for its main results. If Yahoo! is now powered by Google, then why bother using it? For one thing, you might find that the way Yahoo! 'enhances' Google's listings with information from its own directory may make search results more readable. In addition, Yahoo!'s search results pages still show 'Directory Category Matches'. When offered, these will take you to a list of websites that have been reviewed and approved by a human editor. It's also possible to do a pure search of just the human-compiled Yahoo! Directory, which is how the old or 'classic' Yahoo! used to work. To do this, search from the Yahoo! Directory homepage, as opposed to the regular Yahoo.com home page. Then you'll get both Directory Category Matches and 'Directory Site Matches', which are the top website matches drawn from all categories of the Yahoo! Directory.

Sites pay a fee to be included in the Yahoo! Directory's commercial listings, though they must meet editor approval before being accepted. Non-commercial content is accepted for free. Consider Yahoo! any time you think you might be well served by having a list of human-reviewed websites. It's also a good choice for popular queries, since the category listings it provides may help you narrow in and refine your query. Doing a pure Yahoo! Directory search also provides a unique human view of the web.

MSN Search[5]

Microsoft is known for constantly reworking its software products until they get them right, and MSN Search is a shining example of the company putting that same effort into an online product. In particular, the company has its own team of editors that monitor the most popular searches being performed and then hand-picks sites that are believed to be the most relevant. After performing a search, 'Popular Topics' shown below the search box on the results page are also suggestions built largely by editors to guide you into making a more refined search. When appropriate, search results may also feature links to encyclopedia content from Microsoft Encarta or news headlines at the top of the page.

Of course, human editors can't do everything, so MSN Search also relies on search providers for answers to many of its queries. Usually, it will be human-powered results from the LookSmart directory that dominate the page. Unlike when MSN editors are involved, these human-powered results are not hand-picked to match a query. Instead, MSN uses its own search algorithm to sift through all the listings from LookSmart to automatically find answers that are believed to be best. (More information about LookSmart is given below.)

Overall, MSN Search provides a blend of human-powered directory information and crawler coverage different from any of the other top choices listed above. It's a high-quality resource that provides its own unique view of the Web and is one worth checking.

Lycos[6]

Lycos is one of the oldest search engines on the Web, launched in 1994. It ceased crawling the Web for its own listings in April 1999 and instead uses crawler-based results provided by FAST (see above). So why bother with Lycos rather than using FAST's own AllTheWeb.com site? One reason is that you might like some of the features that Lycos provides. 'Fast Forward' lets you see search results on one side of your screen and the actual pages listed in another. Relevant categories of human-compiled information from the Open Directory appear at the bottom of the search results page. At the top of the page, Lycos will suggest other searches related to your original topic right under the search box. On the other hand, you might even like the look and feel better! Whatever the reason, under the hood, Lycos provides all the same relevancy and comprehensiveness you'll find at AllTheWeb.com.

Ask Jeeves[7]

Ask Jeeves initially gained fame in 1998 and 1999 as being the 'natural language' search engine that let you search by asking questions and responded with what seemed to be the right answer to everything. In reality, technology wasn't what made Ask Jeeves perform so well. Behind the scenes, the company at one point had about 100 editors who monitored search logs. They then went out onto the Web and located what seemed to be the best sites to match the most popular queries.

Humans are still used at Ask Jeeves, though the number of editors is now only around ten. Nevertheless, the human-provided answers may still be the selling point for why some people, especially those new to the Web, may want to use Ask Jeeves. For popular queries, the human-selected matches in the 'Click Ask below for your answers' sections of the results may feel very relevant. If shown, these appear at the very top and bottom of the search results page.

Besides humans, Ask Jeeves also uses crawler-based technology to provide results to its users. These results come from the Teoma search engine which it owns and which is described below.

AOL Search[8]

AOL Search provides users with editorial listings that come from Google's crawler-based index. Indeed, the same search on Google and AOL Search will come up with very similar matches. So, why would you use AOL Search? Primarily because you are an AOL user. The 'internal' version of AOL Search provides links to content only available within the AOL online service. In this way, you can search AOL and the entire Web at the same time. The 'external' version lacks these links. Why wouldn't you use AOL Search? If you like Google, many of Google's features such as 'cached' pages are not offered by AOL Search.

Teoma[9]

Teoma is a crawler-based search engine owned by Ask Jeeves. It has an extremely small index of the Web, only about one-tenth the size of crawler-competitors Google, AllTheWeb.com, Inktomi and AltaVista. However, being large doesn't make much of a difference when it comes to popular queries, and Teoma has won praise for its relevancy since it appeared in 2000. Some people also like its 'Refine' feature, which offers suggested topics to explore after you do a search. The 'Resources' section of results is also unique, pointing users to pages that specifically serve as link resources about various topics. Teoma was purchased by Ask Jeeves in September 2001 and also provides some results to that website.

WiseNut[10]

Like Teoma, WiseNut is a crawler-based search engine that attracted attention when it appeared on the scene in 2001. Like Teoma, WiseNut features good relevancy. Unlike Teoma, WiseNut has a large database, making it nearly as comprehensive as Google, AllTheWeb.com and Inktomi.

However, the WiseNut database has not been refreshed since June 2001. This incredible staleness should have been corrected in late 2002, when WiseNut's owner LookSmart was promising to revamp the engine. LookSmart bought WiseNut in April 2002. If the revamp ever takes place, then WiseNut may deliver on its initial promise.

Inktomi[11]

Inktomi is unusual in that it is the only major search engine in this listing that does not offer its own search site. If you go to the Inktomi site given here, you'll only find company information, not the ability to search the Web. Instead, Inktomi prefers to be solely a 'behind-the-scenes' partner for other search engines that need results, such as MSN Search.

Among the major search engines, Inktomi is the second-oldest crawler. It briefly operated as an experimental search engine at UC Berkeley. However, the creators then formed their own company in 1996 with the same name and gained their first customer, HotBot, in the middle of that year. Today, Inktomi continues to crawl the Web. The company had been left behind by rivals Google and AllTheWeb.com in terms of comprehensiveness, but changes made in the summer of 2002 have made it much more competitive.

In March 2003 Yahoo! announced the acquisition of Inktomi Corp. A feature offered on the new website is billed as 'index freshness', described as a reflection of the frequency of updates to the search index. Inktomi web search refreshes the entire index every 10–14 days.

LookSmart[12]

LookSmart is a human-compiled directory of websites. The company does operate its own website, but this really isn't intended for the public to use. Instead, similar to Inktomi,

LookSmart provides its results to other search engines that need listings.

LookSmart gathers its listings in two ways. Commercial sites pay to be listed in its commercial categories, making the service very much like an electronic 'Yellow Pages'. There are also volunteer editors at the LookSmart-owned Zeal directory (*http://www.zeal.com*) who catalogue non-commercial sites into this non-commercial directory.

LookSmart launched independently in October 1996, was backed by Reader's Digest for about a year, and then company executives bought back control of the service.

Open Directory[13]

The Open Directory uses volunteer editors to catalogue the Web. Formerly known as NewHoo, it was launched in June 1998. It was acquired by the AOL Time Warner-owned Netscape in November 1998, and the company pledged that anyone would be able to use information from the directory through an open licence arrangement.

While you can search at the Open Directory site itself, this is not recommended. The site has no 'backup' results that kick in should there not be a match in the human-compiled database. In addition, the ranking of sites during keyword searching is poor, while alphabetical ordering is used when you choose to 'browse' categories by topic.

Instead, to scan the valuable information compiled by the Open Directory, consider using the version offered by Google, the Google Directory. Here, keyword searching uses Google's refined relevancy algorithms and makes use of link analysis to better propel good pages from the human database to the top. In addition, when viewing sites by category, they will be listed in 'PageRank' order, which means the most popular sites based on analysing links from across the Web will be listed first.

Overture[14]

Formerly called GoTo until late 2001, Overture is an extremely popular paid placement search engine that provides ads to many of the search engines listed above.

How does a search engine work?

The results of a search engine are built by computer robot programs, not by human selection. A search engine is not organised by subject categories; all pages are ranked by a computer algorithm. It is helpful to remember that the results contain the full text (every word) of the web pages they link to. The database of a search engine is huge and queries often retrieve a lot of information. Most search engines therefore allow you to search within results, which is especially useful for complex searches. The results are not evaluated – this has to be done by the user.

Before you type in your search question, it is advisable to think about where and what to try first, how many search engines to try and at what point you will quit.

My first try is almost always with a simple search engine. Easy Searcher 2[15] has a good collection of subject-specific search engines. They offer search engines and also directories for the following categories:

- WWW Engines

- Desktop Reference

- Entertainment

- Health/Medicine

- News/Weather

- Social/Political

- Arts/Humanities/Languages

- Education

- Food/Drink

- History/Archaeology

- Publications/Literature

- Software

- Travel

- Business/Finance/Employment

- Engineering/Chemical/Maths

- Government/Law

- Internet Resources

- Science/Nature/Environment

- Sports/Recreation/Hobbies/Pets.

Each category has links to various relevant resources, directories and search engines.

My strategy with search engines, especially if I am not very sure what exactly I am looking for, is as follows:

- Do what seems obvious first. Just type in the first word that comes to mind. If you are looking for information on Whistler, enter 'Whistler' rather than 'painters'. Make your keywords as specific as possible. 'Bordeaux Chateau Latour' gets more relevant results than 'good French claret'.

■ Don't be intimidated. Type in a single or several keywords.

■ Do not bother with advanced search techniques at the beginning of your search.

■ Start with a simple search. You can always refine it later.

■ Use quotation marks to perform a phrase search. For example, to search for the book 'A Woman in White', use quotations around the entire phrase in the right order.

Being able to use quotation marks is search engine-specific and not all search engines offer this possibility. (Moreover, in this book the style is to use single quote marks, but check with the search engine you are using whether single or double quotes are required.) Here again, if you are comfortable with a particular search engine, get to know their particular search hints. Once you are used to it, it will become natural and you will not even think about adding quotation marks if you are looking for a particular phrase.

When you are happy with your search words, hit the Enter button and see what comes back. Probably, you will get far too many results. Do not let this intimidate you.

Look at the first ten only, and read the snippets. Do not yet open the new pages. Just look at the information that is available there. This will give you a feel for the subject and it will also tell you whether you are on the right track. As you continue to search, keep rethinking your search arguments. What new approaches could you use? Are you using the right words? What are some related subjects to search for that might lead you to the one you really want?

Some years ago, the online databases used a structured query language like Boolean logic and more recently SQL (Structured Query Language). A professional could learn this logic language and apply it to control the search. These languages and the resulting hits were 100 per cent logic and they brought back exactly what one asked for. In order to obtain good results, it was necessary to know the query language well.

Today, the technology behind the search engines has been optimised so that laypersons are able to get good results. In order to get good results, the layperson does not have to know any logic query language. This means that, theoretically, the layperson gets the same search results as the professional. Today it is in most cases enough to type in the obvious and get good results. Google even lets you make typing errors and the search engine automatically suggests:

Did you mean: Meteorological office
Your search – Meteorollogical office – did not match any documents.

And let us not forget the speed with which the search engines bring back the results. I am still, after almost eight years, constantly amazed at the speed and also at the improvements that are made.

In my opinion, it does not matter so much which search engine you use. What matters is that you feel comfortable with the one you use on a daily basis. Of course, well-known, commercially-backed search engines generally mean more dependable results. They are more likely to be well-maintained and upgraded when necessary.

Basic search engine strategies

Most search engines usually require the same basic search techniques as outlined below and the examples given are generally applicable to them all. A typical example may look like this:

> Sometimes, you want to make sure that a search engine finds pages that have all the words you enter, not just some of them. The + symbol lets you do this:
>
> +windows+98+bugs
>
> Only pages that contain both words would appear in your results.

That's what the manuals say, anyway. Let us test this example. I used Google and first did a search with the + symbol, and then used exactly the same words but without the + symbol.
Google gave me back the following results:

> Query: +windows +98 +bugs
> Results:
>
> Annoyances.org
> Solutions and help for common Windows 95/98 problems, with several discussion forums.
> *www.annoyances.org/*
>
> ZDNet: Windows 98 Bugs
> Check Prices. Windows Product Guide. Office Suites & Productivity. Utilities Guide. Windows 98 Bugs. From ZDNet Reviews & Solutions June 1, 1999...

www.zdnet.com/zdhelp/stories/main/0,5594,2...

ZDNet: Windows 98 Bugs

Windows Product Guide. Office Suites & Productivity. Utilities Guide. Windows 98 Internet Bugs. From ZDNet Reviews & Solutions June 1, 1999...
www.zdnet.com/zdhelp/stories/main/0,5594,2...

Windows 98 bugs and fixes

Windows 98 Bugs and Fixes. I have to hand it to 'Windows Magazine' *http://www.winmag.com/* It's a goldmine of information.
www.geocities.com/Athens/Troy/6883/98bugs...

Query: Windows 98 bugs
Results:

Annoyances.org

Solutions and help for common Windows 95/98 problems, with several discussion forums.
www.annoyances.org/

ZDNet: Windows 98 Bugs

Check Prices. Windows Product Guide. Office Suites & Productivity. Utilities Guide. Windows 98 Bugs. From ZDNet Reviews & Solutions June 1, 1999...
www.zdnet.com/zdhelp/stories/main/0,5594,2...

ZDNet: Windows 98 Bugs

Windows Product Guide. Office Suites & Productivity. Utilities Guide. Windows 98 Internet Bugs. From ZDNet Reviews & Solutions June 1, 1999...
www.zdnet.com/zdhelp/stories/main/0,5594,2...

Windows 98 bugs and fixes

Windows 98 Bugs and Fixes. I have to hand it to 'Windows Magazine' http://www.winmag.com/ It's a goldmine of information.

www.geocities.com/Athens/Troy/6883/98bugs...

As you can see, both queries gave me exactly the same result. ZDNet is a commercial information technology portal, their catchphrase being 'where technology means business'. The page with the Geocities address is a personal, critical collection. The page annoyances.org site will be evaluated in Chapter 5.

In this example, I think it would have been more efficient and better to take the direct approach (search methods 3 and 7) and to ask: who would have this particular information? Most probably the maker of Windows software itself, Microsoft. Microsoft can be found directly at *http://www.microsoft.com*. On the first page, there is an internal search engine. Type in 'Windows 98 bugs' and you are directly pointed to the *Windows 98 and Windows ME Error Message Resource Center.* This a database maintained by Microsoft engineers, collecting all the errors in their software along with solutions to them. All you have to do now is choose your operating system and the error message, and a list of the Microsoft Knowledge Base articles that are available for that error message appears. You can then select the Knowledge Base article that applies to your issue.

Let us look at another example. I tried the search engine Teoma (*http://www.teoma.com*) and typed in the following search query:

the who

This is what the search engine gave back:

> *The Who Concert Guide: The Who live on Stage 1963–2001*
> *The Who Concerts Guide: The Who live on stage 1963–2000...*
> *www.thewho.net/ConcertGuide/*
>
> *The Hypertext Who*
> *The Hypertext Who at thewho.net – A Celebration of the music of The Who...*
> *www.thewho.net/*
> *[More results from www.thewho.net]*
>
> *Jack's The Who page*
> *Jack's, 'The Who' Home Page. Welcome to my home page which centers around one of the greatest rock & roll bands of all time, The Who.*
> *www.riverdale.k12.or.us/students/jackr/who...*
>
> *Welcome to Petetownshend.com*
> *Dec 5: Uncut Magazine 32 page special on The Who – see Who news pages Dec 6: Pete on Uncut article – See Pete's Diaries.*
> *www.petetownshend.com/*

When I searched for

+the +who

this is what I got back:

The Who Concerts Guide: The Who live on Stage 1963–2001
The Who Concerts Guide: The Who live on stage 1963–2000...
www.thewho.net/ConcertGuide/

The Hypertext Who
The Hypertext Who at thewho.net – A Celebration of the music of The Who...
www.thewho.net/

eelpie.com
Scoop 3 DAD and Another Scoop Quiex SV Super Vinyl now available – see music section Aug / Sept: The Who 'Encore' series now available – for...
www.eelpie.com/

Jack's The Who page
Jack's, 'The Who' Home Page. Welcome to my home page which centers around one of the greatest rock & roll bands of all time, The Who.
www.riverdale.k12.or.us/students/jackr/who...

Then I activated

'search for this phrase' **the who**

and got the following answer:

The Who Concerts Guide: The Who live on Stage 1963–2001
The Who Concerts Guide: The Who live on stage 1963–2000...
www.thewho.net/ConcertGuide/

The Hypertext Who

The Hypertext Who at thewho.net – A Celebration of the music of The Who…

www.thewho.net/

[More results from www.thewho.net]

Jack's The Who page

Jack's, 'The Who' Home Page. Welcome to my home page which centers around one of the greatest rock & roll bands of all time, The Who.

www.riverdale.k12.or.us/students/jackr/who…

Welcome to Petetownshend.com

Dec 5: Uncut Magazine 32 page special on The Who – see Who news pages Dec 6: Pete on Uncut article – See Pete's Diaries.

www.petetownshend.com/

When I searched with **'the who'** the result was (by now you can guess) the following:

The Who Concerts Guide: The Who live on Stage 1963–2001

The Who Concerts Guide: The Who live on stage 1963–2000…

www.thewho.net/ConcertGuide/

The Hypertext Who

The Hypertext Who at thewho.net – A Celebration of the music of The Who…

www.thewho.net/

[More results from www.thewho.net]

Jack's The Who page

Jack's, 'The Who' Home Page. Welcome to my home page which centers around one of the greatest rock & roll bands of all time, The Who.

www.riverdale.k12.or.us/students/jackr/who...

Welcome to Petetownshend.com

Dec 5: Uncut Magazine 32 page special on The Who – see Who news pages Dec 6: Pete on Uncut article – See Pete's Diaries.

www.petetownshend.com/

This example shows very well that with popular, well-known search terms what you type in does not really matter that much. It is not even necessary to use the + sign or ' '. However, it is an altogether different matter if you are after scientific or technical information that is completely reliable.

Search engines are particularly useful when you want to:

- find out quickly if any information exists on a specific subject;
- find concrete information on products or persons;
- find products or information of which you have heard or know that there is something on them on the Internet.

On the other hand, directories are particularly useful if you want:

- to get a general overview of the various and many offers on the Web;
- to get an overview of a certain subject;

- to get information on a broader view, e.g. a comparison of various offers on the same subject or in the same field.

An example of a search engine: Google

In the following pages I will focus on Google (at the time of writing the acknowledged market leader) to show how a search engine works in detail.

Many search engines return results based on how often keywords appear in a website. Google is different. They have developed an advanced search technology called PageRank™, which involves a series of simultaneous calculations typically occurring in under half a second, without human intervention. Their search architecture is also scalable, which enables them to continue to index the Internet as it grows.

The intention is to perform an objective measurement of the importance of web pages. Google does not count links; instead it uses the vast link structure of the Web as an organisational tool. In essence, Google interprets a link from page A to page B as a 'vote' by page A for page B. The importance of a page is therefore assessed by the votes it receives. The pages that cast the votes are then analysed. Votes cast by pages that are themselves 'important' weigh more heavily and help to make other pages important, thus important, high-quality pages receive a higher PageRank and are ordered or ranked higher in the results. In this way Google's technology uses the collective intelligence of the Web to determine a page's importance. Google does not use editors or its own employees to judge a page's importance. In my opinion, this is one of the advantages of this technology – I feel I can trust this technology because it makes sense and seems to be a good way of judging the importance of web pages. If the same work was done by people I would always have to ask myself: are they biased towards one page or the other?

Google has many special services and tools to help you find the answers you are looking for. One of the main differences between a layman and a professional is that the professional always reads the manual. The professional realises from experience that the time it takes to read the help pages will be time saved later on.

The basics of a Google search given below are taken from the Google website.

The basics of Google search

To enter a query into Google, just type in a few descriptive words and hit the Enter key (or click on the Google Search button) for a list of relevant web pages. Since Google only returns web pages that contain *all* the words in your query, refining or narrowing your search is as simple as adding more words to the search terms you have already entered. Your new query will return a smaller subset of the pages Google found for your original query that was too broad.

Choosing keywords

For best results, it's important to choose your keywords wisely. Keep these tips in mind:

1   Try the obvious first. If you're looking for information on Picasso, enter 'Picasso' rather than 'painters'.

2   Use words likely to appear on a site with the information you want. 'Luxury hotel Dubuque' gets better results than 'really nice places to spend the night in Dubuque'.

3   Make keywords as specific as possible. 'Antique lead soldiers' gets more relevant results than 'old metal toys'.

Automatic 'and' queries

By default, Google only returns pages that include all of your search terms. There is no need to include 'and' between terms. Keep in mind that the order in which the terms are typed will affect the search results. To restrict a search further, just include more terms. For example, to plan a vacation to Hawaii, simply type:

vacation hawaii	Google Search

Automatic exclusion of common words

Google ignores common words and characters such as 'where' and 'how', as well as certain single digits and single letters, because they tend to slow down your search without improving the results. Google will indicate if a common word has been excluded by displaying details on the results page below the search box.

If a common word is essential to getting the results you want, you can include it by putting a '+' sign in front of it. (Be sure to include a space before the '+' sign.) Another method for doing this is conducting a phrase search, which simply means putting quotation marks around two or more words. Common words in a phrase search (e.g. 'where are you') are included in the search. For example, to search for Star Wars, Episode I, use:

Star Wars Episode +1	Google Search

or

"Star Wars Episode 1"	Google Search

Capitalisation

Google searches are *not* case sensitive. All letters, regardless of how you type them, will be understood as lower case. For example, searches for 'george washington', 'George Washington', and 'gEoRgE wAsHiNgToN' will all return the same results.

Word variations (stemming)

To provide the most accurate results, Google does not use 'stemming' or support 'wildcard' searches. In other words, Google searches for exactly the words that you enter in the search box. Searching for 'googl' or 'googl*' will not yield 'googler' or 'googlin'. If in doubt, try both forms: 'airline' and 'airlines', for instance.

Search by category

The Google Web Directory[16] is a good place to start if you're not exactly sure which search keywords to use. For example, searching for [Saturn] within the Science > Astronomy category of the Google Web Directory returns only pages about the planet Saturn, while searching for [Saturn] within the automotive category returns only pages about Saturn cars. Searching within a category of interest allows you to quickly pinpoint the most relevant pages to you.

Advanced search made easy

You can increase the accuracy of your searches by adding operators that fine-tune your keywords. Most of the options listed below can be entered directly into the Google search box or selected from Google's 'Advanced Search page' (see Figure 4.1).

Figure 4.1 Google Advanced Search page

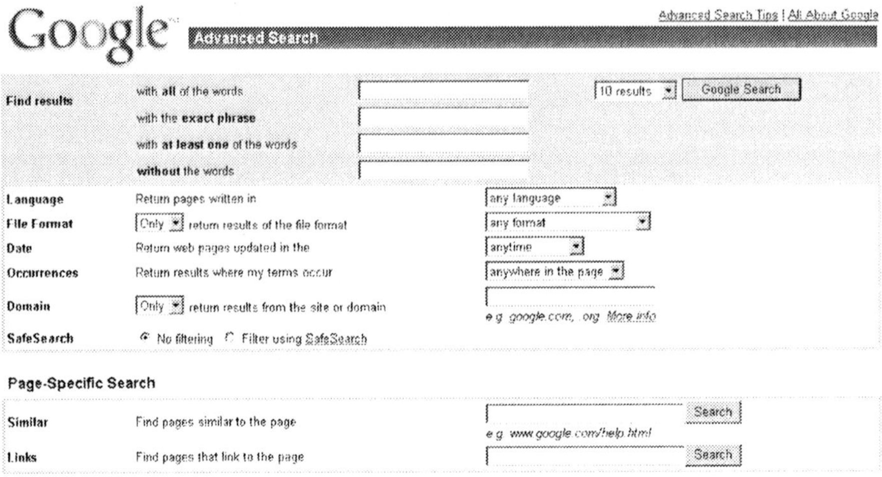

Additionally, Google supports several *advanced operators* which are query words that have special meaning to Google. For a complete list, see below.

' + ' searches

Google ignores common words and characters such as 'where' and 'how', as well as certain single digits and single letters, because they tend to slow down your search without improving the results. Google will indicate if a common word has been excluded by displaying details on the results page below the search box. If a common word is essential to getting the results you want, you can include it by putting a '+' sign in front of it. (Be sure to include a space before the '+' sign.)

Another method for doing this is conducting a phrase search, which simply means putting quotation marks around two or more words. Common words in a phrase search (e.g. 'where are you') are included in the search.

' - ' searches

Sometimes what you're searching for has more than one meaning, for example 'bass' can refer to fishing or music. You can exclude a word from your search by putting a minus sign ('-') immediately in front of the term you want to avoid. (Be sure to include a space before the minus sign.) For example, to find web pages about bass that do not contain the word 'music', type:

bass -music	Google Search

Phrase searches

Search for complete phrases by enclosing them in quotation marks. Words enclosed in double quotes ("like this") will appear together in all results exactly as you have entered them. Phrase searches are especially useful when searching for famous sayings or proper names.

'OR' searches

Google supports the logical 'OR' operator. To retrieve pages that include either word A or word B, use an uppercase OR between terms. For example, to search for a vacation in either London or Paris, just type:

vacation london OR paris	Google Search

Domain restrict

If you know the website you want to search but aren't sure where the information is located within that site, you can use Google to search only that domain. Do this by entering what you're looking for followed by the word 'site' and a colon followed by the domain name. For example, to find admission information on Stanford University's site, enter:

admission site:www.stanford.edu	Google Search

Other advanced search features

- **Language:** specify which language you would like your results returned in.

- **Date:** restrict your results to the past three, six or 12 months.

- **Occurrences:** specify where your search terms occur on the page – anywhere on the page, in the title, or in the URL.

- **Domains:** search only a specific website or exclude that site completely from your search.

- **SafeSearch:** Google's SafeSearch screens for sites that contain this type of information and eliminates them from search results.

Figure 4.2 shows the results of a Google search. Each letter corresponds to the explanations provided below.

Figure 4.2 Google search results

A **Advanced Search:** links to a page that enables you to restrict your search if necessary.

B **Preferences:** links to a page that enables you to set search preferences, including the default number of results per page, the interface language and whether to screen results using the SafeSearch filter.

C **Language Tools:** tools for setting language preferences for pages to be searched, interface language and translation of results.

D **Search Tips:** links to information that will help you search more effectively. Tells you how Google differs from other search engines – from the way it handles basic queries to the special features that set it apart.

E **Search field:** to enter a query into Google, just type in a few descriptive keywords. Hit Enter or click on the Google Search button for your list of relevant results.

F **Google Search button:** click on this button to submit another search query. You can also submit a query by hitting the Enter key.

G **Tabs:** click the tab for the kind of search you want to conduct. Choose from a full web search, images only, Google Groups (Usenet discussion archive) or the Google Directory (the Web organised into browsable categories).

H **Statistics bar:** this line describes your search and indicates the number of results returned as well as the amount of time it took to complete your search.

I **Category:** if your search terms also appear in the web directory, these suggested categories may help you find more information related to your query. Click on them to browse for other links.

J   **Page title:** the first line of the result is the title of the web page found. Sometimes, instead of a title there will be a URL, meaning that either the page has no title, or Google has not indexed the full content of that page. It is still a good match because of other web pages – which have been indexed – that have links to this returned page. If the text associated with these links matches your query, the page may be returned as a result even though its full text has not been indexed.

K   **Text below the title:** this text is an excerpt from the returned result page with your query terms emboldened. These excerpts let you see the context in which your search terms appear on the page, before you click on the result.

L   **Description:** if your search query is listed in the web directory, the description filed by the open directory author is displayed.

M   **Category:** if a site found by your search query is listed in the web directory, the category in which it appears is displayed below its description.

N   **URL of result:** this is the web address of the returned result.

O   **Size:** this number is the size of the text portion of the found web page. It is omitted for sites that have not yet been indexed.

P   **Cached:** clicking the cached link will enable you to see the contents of the web page as of the time it was indexed. If for some reason the site link does not connect you to the current page, you can still retrieve the cached version and may find the information you need there. Your search terms are highlighted on the cached version.

Q **Similar pages:** when you select the similar pages link for a particular result, Google automatically scouts the web for pages that are related to this result.

R **Indented result:** when Google finds multiple results from the same website, the most relevant result is listed first with the other relevant pages from that same site indented below it.

S **More results:** if there are more than two results from the same site, the remaining results can be accessed by clicking on 'More results from...' link.

Customise your results using the preferences page

Google enables you to save certain search preferences, including the number of results to show per page, the interface language and whether or not to use SafeSearch filtering.

Interface language

Google puts the 'World' in 'World Wide Web' with their multi-language search service. It is possible to set your Google homepage, the message and the buttons to display in your native language. This can be done by saving your preferences. Google currently offers the following languages:

Afrikaans	German	Persian
Albanian	Greek	Pig Latin
Amharic	Gujarati	Polish
Arabic	Hacker	Portuguese
Azerbaijani	Hebrew	Portuguese (Portugal)
Basque	Hindi	Punjabi
Belarusian	Hungarian	Romanian
Bengali	Icelandic	Russian
Bihari	Indonesian	Scots Gaelic
Bork, bork, bork!	Interlingua	Serbian
Bosnian	Irish	Sinhalese
Bulgarian	Italian	Slovak
Catalan	Japanese	Slovenian
Chinese (Simplified)	Javanese	Spanish
Chinese (Traditional)	Kannada	Sundanese
Croatian	Klingon	Swahili
Czech	Korean	Swedish
Danish	Latin	Tagalog
Dutch	Latvian	Tamil
Elmer Fudd	Lithuanian	Telugu
English	Macedonian	Thai
Esperanto	Malay	Tigrinya
Estonian	Malayalam	Turkish
Faroese	Maltese	Ukrainian
Finnish	Marathi	Urdu
French	Nepali	Uzbek
Frisian	Norwegian	Vietnamese
Galician	Norwegian (Nynorsk)	Welsh
Georgian	Occitan	

Web page translation

Google breaks the language barrier with this translation feature. Using machine translation technology, Google now gives English speakers access to a variety of non-English web pages. This feature is currently available for pages published in Italian, French, Spanish, German and Portuguese.

If your search has non-English results, there will be a link to a version of that page translated into English.

Search language

Google's language search feature lets you restrict your searches to pages in the language(s) that you choose. Because these language-restricted searches only look at pages from a small portion of the Web, however, Google recommends the 'Search web pages written in any language' option as a default. Specifying a search language can be quite useful, however, when you want to search for content that is specific to a particular language or region.

Number of results

Google's default setting of 10 provides the fastest results. However, you can increase the number or results displayed per page to 20, 30, 50 or 100.

New results window

If you prefer to retain the main Google search page, check this preference box to open your results in a new browser window.

SafeSearch filtering

Many Google users prefer not to have adult sites included in their search results. Google's SafeSearch screens for sites that contain pornography and explicit sexual content and eliminates them from search results. While no filter is 100 per cent accurate, Google's filter uses advanced proprietary technology that checks keywords and phrases, URLs and Open Directory categories.

By default, *moderate filtering* is set to exclude most explicit images from Google Image Search results. To apply Google's SafeSearch filtering to both web search and image search results, select the *strict filtering* option on the web search preferences page and save your preferences. This will activate stricter filtering of images, as well as filtering of adult content in regular Google search results. To *turn off filtering* completely, select the 'do not filter...' option. The filtering option you select on the preferences page will remain on until you change and resave your preferences. You can also adjust your SafeSearch settings on the 'Advanced Search' or the 'Advanced Image Search' pages on a per search basis. Google strives to keep the filtering information as current and comprehensive as possible through continual crawling of the Web and by incorporating updates from user suggestions. I would recommend strongly that, if you find sites that contain offensive content in your results, even with SafeSearch activated, you send an e-mail with the site's URL to Google. Only if we react may they investigate.

Google services and tools

Google has many special services and tools to help you to find exactly what you're looking for. The most recently added services are Froogle and Google News.

Google services

- *Froogle (froogle.google.com)* – find products for sale from across the Web.

- *Google Answers (answers.google.com)* – an open forum where researchers answer your questions for a fee.

- *Google Catalogs (catalogs.google.com)* – search and browse mail-order catalogues online.

- *Google Groups (groups.google.com)* – post and read comments in Usenet discussion forums.

- *Google Image Search (images.google.com)* – the most comprehensive image search on the Web with 390 million images.

- *Google Labs (labs.google.com)* – prototypes and projects in development by Google engineers, including: Google Viewer, Google WebQuotes, Google Glossary, Google Sets, Voice Search, Keyboard Shortcuts.

- *Google News (news.google.com)* – search and browse 4,000 continuously updated news sources.

- *Google Special Searches (www.google.com/options/specialsearches.html)* – narrow your search to a specific topic, such as BSD, Apple and Microsoft.

- *Google University Search (www.google.com/options/universities.html)* – narrow your search to a specific school website.

- *Google Web Directory (directory.google.com)* – the Web organised by topic into categories.

- *Google Web Search (www.google.com)* – fast relevant results from searching more than 3 billion web pages.

- *Google Wireless (www.google.com/options/wireless.html)* – access Google's adaptable search technology from any number of handheld devices.

Google tools

- *Google Browser Buttons (www.google.com/options/buttons.html)* – access Google's search technology by adding our buttons to your browser's personal toolbar.

- *Google in Your Language (services.google.com/tc/Welcome.html)* – volunteer to translate Google's help information and search interface into your favourite language.

- *Google Toolbar (toolbar.google.com)* – take the power of Google with you by adding the toolbar to your IE browser.

- *Google Translate Tool (www.google.com/language_tools)* – translate text or entire web pages.

- *Google Web APIs (www.google.com/apis/)* – a tool for software developers to automatically query Google.

Example: *popular search terms*

You would like to read something on John Nash, the 1994 Nobel Prize winner, because you have just seen *A Beautiful Mind*. This is a simple search where an ordinary search engine is quite sufficient. It is safe to assume that 'John Nash' has become a popular search term since the Hollywood movie.

Type in John Nash (with or without quote marks) and this is the result with Google:

---

1. *http://www.nobel.se/economics/laureates/1994/nash -autobio.html*

This is the official autobiography of John Nash on the website of the Nobel Institute

2. *http://www.nobel.se/economics/laureates/1994*

This is the official Nobel Institute site of the 1994 prize winners in Economics

3. *http://www-gap.dcs-st-and.ac.uk/~history/ Mathematicians/Nash.html*

This is the personal interest website of a student studying at the University of St Andrews

4. *http://cepa.newschool.edu/het/profiles/nash.htm*

This is a site on John Nash on the page of the History of Economic Thought, maintained by students at the Johns Hopkins University and the New School University in New York. This site also has links to further resources.

5. *http://www.pbs.org/wgbh/amex/nash*

Information on a documentary done by the Public Broadcasting Service in the US. Includes much background information and many links.

There is no need to perform further searches.

Meta search engines

Even the best search engine can only cover a small part of the whole Internet. Nobody knows how big the World Wide Web actually is. It is estimated that there are more than 500 billion pages. And these pages change almost every day – pages are deleted every day, new pages are added, existing pages are updated. Therefore, there is no single search engine that comes even close to searching the whole Web. If a query with a single search engine does not yield the hoped-for results, it may be a good idea to try the search with a meta search engine. Meta search engines simultaneously search multiple search engines. Sometimes, they are also referred to as parallel search engines or multi-threaded search engines. Meta search engines may turn out to be useful in the following situations:

- when researching an obscure topic;
- when you are not having luck finding anything when you search;
- when you want to retrieve a relatively small number of relevant results.

A meta search engine does not search the Web itself, but it uses the data and the services of other search engines and displays them in a new form. A search typed into a meta search engine is sent on to the collaborating search engines. This is done very fast, because most meta search engines have a special back-door opening to the other search engines. There are then two ways a meta search engine displays the search results.

By one method, the user gets the same results as if he had searched all the search engines separately, only faster. One type searches a number of engines and does not collate the results. This means you must look through a separate list of results from each engine that was searched so you will often see the same result more than once. Some engines require you to visit each site to view your results, while others will fetch the results back to their own sites. When results are brought back to the site, a certain limitation is placed on what is allowed to be retrieved. With this type of meta search engine, you can retrieve comprehensive, and sometimes overwhelming, results.

By the second method, the meta crawlers take the results from the separate search engines and process them using their own logic system. For example, the results may be assessed, put in a new order or have added notes. The user gets therefore more than the sum of the collected results. This type is more common and returns a single list of results, often with the duplicate hits removed. This type of meta engine always brings the results back to its own site for viewing. In these cases, the engine retrieves a certain maximum number of documents from the individual engines it has searched, cut off after a certain point as the search is processed. The cut-off may be determined by the number of documents retrieved or by the amount of time the meta engine spends at the other sites. Some of these services give the user a certain degree of control over these factors. All of this has two implications:

- These meta search engines return only a portion of the documents available to be retrieved from the individual engines they have searched.
- Results retrieved by these engines can be highly relevant, since they are usually grabbing the first items from the list of hits ranked by relevancy returned by the individual search engines.

Metacrawler

At the time of writing, Metacrawler[17] is usually cited as the most efficient and most popular meta search engine. Metacrawler also offers a web directory. The main headings of their directory are:

- Arts & Entertainment
- Autos
- Business & Money
- Computers & Internet
- Games
- Health
- News & Media
- Recreation
- Reference
- Regional
- Science & Technology
- Society
- Sports
- Travel.

Metacrawler advertise themselves by saying: 'Get the most relevant results you are looking for fast by searching multiple search engines at once'. The 'advanced search' allows the setting of 'keyword default' (search for any of the supplied words, all of the words or the exact phrase provided). The user can indicate which search engines should be searched by the crawler. It is also possible to choose the number of results to be displayed on each page and the maximum number of results from each engine. The results can either be sorted by relevance or source (where source means search engine). The maximum amount of time to wait for results can also be chosen.

WebCrawler

WebCrawler[18] users understand the value of searching the Web, according to WebCrawler's own text. It tells us that 'by searching with WebCrawler you get to search multiple search engines at once'. It claims that their technology highlights the strengths of many of the Web's major search properties, 'delivering more relevant and comprehensive results every time'. WebCrawler searches commercial and non-commercial sources.

Dogpile

Dogpile[19] offers exactly the same web directory as Metacrawler. Additionally, it offers the 'joke of the day' and claims to get the results twice as fast as before.

Meta crawlers are not always the better choice when searching the Web. Most of them only allow simple search terms; more complicated requests cannot be processed. Searches for very popular terms, for example, usually yield the same results from each of the different search engines so the use of a meta search engine is unnecessary. In my experience, I have hardly ever found it necessary to resort to a meta crawler. I have almost always found what I was looking for by simple searches with one search engine or via directories.

Directories

An alternative to using a search engine is to explore a structured directory of topics. A directory is an approach to organising information – a link collection, hierarchically ordered into categories. The most familiar example of a directory is the telephone directory. On the Web, a directory is typically organised by major topics. Well-known directories are those at Yahoo! and Google. A number of Web portal sites offer both the search engine and directory approaches to finding information. Sometimes, the term directory is used synonymously with subject gateway or portal.

An increasing number of universities, libraries, companies, organisations and even volunteers are creating subject directories to catalogue large parts of the Web. These directories are organised by subject and consist of links to Internet resources relating to these subjects. The major subject directories available on the Web tend to have overlapping but different databases. Most directories provide a search capability that allows you to query the database on your topic of interest.

Directories may be useful if you are researching general topics or if you would like to explore a specific topic. Directories also come into their own if you just want to do a bit of browsing. I also find them helpful if I do not know the subject that I am researching. The browsing of directories might give you an idea of what exactly you are looking for.

There are two basic types of directories: academic and professional directories often created and maintained by subject experts to support the needs of researchers, and directories contained on commercial portals that cater to the general public and are competing for traffic. Be sure you use the directory that appropriately meets your needs. Academic directories are usually the result of many years of intellectual effort.

The bigger a directory the more difficult it can be to divide the categories and to add new entries consistent with the existing ones. Added to this comes the fact that every directory does not have the same categories; sometimes they differ slightly. Would you, for example, search for the online version of a sports magazine under the heading of 'Sports' or rather 'Media'? In some cases, several attempts may be necessary to find the subcategory where a page has been placed. And editor X might put a sports magazine in category 'Sports' while editor Y would put it under 'Media'.

Searching for key words in directories might be the solution. Most directories allow a word search within their database. Enter a search term and the results will soon show you where they and similar subjects where placed. Choose the appropriate category from there and explore it. Such keyword searching within directories is a tool worth considering.

Subject directories differ significantly in selectivity. Commercial directories usually do not have a careful evaluation of user-submitted content. It is therefore not a reliable research source and should not be used for this purpose. Consider the policies of any directory that you visit. One challenge to this is the fact that not all directory services are willing to disclose either their policies or the names and qualifications of site reviewers. A number of subject directories consist of links accompanied by annotations that describe or evaluate site content. A well-written annotation from a known reviewer may be more useful than an annotation written by the site creator, as is the case with some directories.

One example of an academic directory is Infomine,[20] a scholarly Internet resource collection. It is a virtual library relevant to faculty, students and research staff at university level. It is maintained by librarians from various American universities and contains Internet resources such as databases, electronic journals, electronic books, bulletin boards, mailing lists, articles and directories of researchers.

Subject gateways, portals and vortals

The terms subject gateway, portal, vortal, megaportal and horizontal enterprise portal are often used synonymously.

Subject gateways and portals

Generally, the term portal is synonymously used for gateway, and stands for a website that is or proposes to be a major starting site for users when they get connected to the Web or that users tend to visit as an anchor site. There are general portals and specialised or niche portals. Some of the more important general portals include Yahoo!,[21] Excite,[22] Netscape,[23] Lycos,[24] Microsoft Network[25] and AOL.[26]

On a professional level, you will probably find little use for commercial portals. For example, the topic list on Lycos starts with the following subjects in this order (!): War coverage, Autos, Blogs, Build a Website, Computers, Download music ... (A blog is short for 'weblog', which is a type of website. Mostly they are in the form of an online journal or diary. Blogs are sometimes chosen instead of a traditional website because they are easier to update, being text-based and no HTML is required.)

A number of large access providers offer portals to the Web for their own users. Most portals have adopted the Yahoo! style of content categories with a text-intensive, faster loading page that visitors find easy to use and do return to. Typical services offered by portal sites include a directory of websites, a facility to search for other sites, news, weather information, e-mail, stock quotes, phone and map information, and sometimes a community forum. Portals differ from vortals (see below) in that they provide a broad range of services and content to a diverse range of customers. They do not seek to target their services to a particular demographic group, industry or topical category. They can therefore be characterised as 'horizontal' in scope as opposed to 'vertical'.

A subject gateway is a website that provides searchable and browsable access to online resources focused around a specific subject. Subject gateway resource descriptions are usually created manually rather than being generated via an automated process. Because the resource entries are generated by hand they are usually superior to those available from conventional web search engines.

A brilliant example of an academic subject gateway is the Resource Discovery Network (RDN).[27] The RDN is a collaboration of over 60 educational and research organisations, including the Natural History Museum and the British Library. In contrast to search engines, the RDN gathers resources that are carefully selected, indexed and described by specialists in partner institutions. This gives the surfer or the researcher the confidence that the search results and browsing will connect to websites that are relevant to learning, teaching and research. The RDN is a cooperative network consisting of a central organisation, the Resource Discovery Network Centre (RDNC), and a number of independent service providers called hubs. The people responsible for the RDN want to further develop the gateway over the next couple of years in order to provide rich, trustworthy and evaluated entry points to a full range of Internet, bibliographic, documentary and data resources. The RDN is freely accessible to all via the Internet.

The so-called hubs provide data for the RDN. They are also services in their own right, providing gateways to Internet resources in their subject areas and often other electronic services too. Hubs may be individual organisations or (more frequently) consortia of prominent library, academic, research and professional organisations. Because the hubs create databases and services for the RDN this means that key activities, such as selection and evaluation of resources, are carried out locally by the people with the necessary expertise and subject knowledge. There are currently six hubs available:

1. ALTIS – Hospitality, Leisure, Sport and Tourism
2. BIOME – Health and Life Sciences

3. EEVL – Engineering, Mathematics and Computing

4. Humbul – Humanities

5. PSIgate – Physical Sciences

6. SOSIG – Social Sciences, Business and Law.

The hubs welcome active participation and your contribution could help create a better resource for the whole academic community. It is also possible to contribute to the development of any hub in one's field of interest by joining in e-mail discussion. Most hubs run lists to which anyone can subscribe.

The Humbul Humanities Hub[28] aims to be the UK's higher and further education's first choice for accessing online humanities resources. The site contains link collections for the following subjects: archaeology, classics, history, philosophy, history and philosophy of science, religion and theology, American studies, humanities computing, linguistics, English studies, German studies, French studies, Spanish studies, Italian studies, Russian and Slavonic studies, and comparative literature.

Another example of a subject gateway is Academic Info,[29] a gateway to quality educational resources, providing students, teachers and librarians with an easy-to-use online subject directory. It is browsable by subject and can also be searched by key words.

Vortals

On the Web, a vortal (vertical industry portal) is a website that provides a gateway or portal to information related to a particular industry such as healthcare, insurance, automobiles or food manufacturing. (A vertical industry is one that is focused on a relatively narrow range of goods and services, whereas a horizontal industry is one that aims to produce a wide range of goods and services. Because most industry tends to specialise, most industry tends to be vertical.) Another term that might also be applied here is *interest community website*, since any vertical industry brings together people sharing an interest in buying, selling or exchanging information about that particular industry. Vortals are also seen as likely business-to-business communities – for example, small business people with home offices might be attracted to a comprehensive vortal that provides ideas and product information related to setting up and maintaining the home office.

An example of a vortal is *http://www.cars.com*, a platform for buying, selling and valuing cars of all makes.

The invisible web

The visible Web is what can be searched and therefore be seen by using search engines and directories. However, the contents of databases rarely show up in search engine results. Search engine spiders cannot or will not go inside database tables and extract the data. Database content is therefore 'invisible' to them. Pages that cannot be found in this fashion are part of the so-called 'invisible web'. Because of the fact that many answers may be found through a simple search with one of the main search engines, we tend to forget that there is also this something variously called the invisible web, the hidden web, the deep web. There are countless hidden treasures out there that cannot be found with conventional search engines. It is estimated that the invisible web is roughly 500 times bigger than the conventional Web. However, it has been argued that the term invisible Web is perhaps a rather poor choice, because it takes the viewpoint that the only way to find information on the Web is to consult a search engine. It assumes that if the information cannot be found on a search engine, it simply is not there, which is of course not the case.

The terms used in a search query are sent into that specialised database, and are returned in another web page that is dynamically generated for your answer. It is not retained anywhere after your search. Search engines cannot access such dynamically generated pages because the computer robots or spiders that build them *cannot type* the searches needed to generate the pages. Spiders find pages by visiting all the links in the pages they 'know about'. Unless there are links somewhere that the spiders can use to regenerate specialised database searches, the contents of the database cannot be reached by the spiders. Pages requiring passwords to access them are also closed to search engines, because spiders cannot type in the required password needed to access the page.

I think that the invisible web gives information professionals a great opportunity to demonstrate that they can add value to an organisation or service by developing an expert knowledge of the invisible web. They will then be able to make use of a much broader range of web resources than most typical Internet searchers.

One easy way to check whether you are on a web page that cannot be found with a conventional search engine is the following trick: have a look at the URL, e.g. *http://www.bertelsmann-stiftung.de/project.cfm?lan=de&nid=33&aid=755*. Now, delete from the end up to and including the question mark, so that the address in the URL field will look like this: *http://www.bertelsmann-stiftung.de/project.cfm* and hit the Enter button. If an error message appears (in this case *Connection failure*) you know that you are on a page that a search engine cannot find.

There is no such thing as recorded information that is invisible. Some information may be more of a challenge to find than others, but this is not the same as invisibility.

Informational databases have been available for years. Many of us are familiar with a library's collection of CD-Roms or web-based research databases. We use online catalogues which are databases of a library's holdings. No one has ever called this information a part of the 'invisible library'. These are simply databases whose content is available through user query. Just like a library, the Web contains information of different types that is stored and retrieved in different ways.

The content of search engines on the Web is itself stored in databases and available only through user query. The whole terminology doesn't seem to be very logical. It is not strictly speaking invisible; it's just that a user query is necessary to find it. The term 'deep web' was first used by a company called BrightPlanet[30] to describe the phenomenon of searchable databases on the Web. (The static web is referred to as the 'surface web'.) This is much better since database content is visible with the appropriate search and retrieval technology.

There are usually considered to be four parts to the invisible web:

- *Almost invisible web*. Conventional search engines index only parts of the whole Web. From a website with roughly 200 pages, only about 50 are indexed; therefore, 150 pages remain in the almost invisible web. This measure is sometimes called the 'depth' of crawling.

- *Gated web*. The gated web consists of pages that require a registration, either with or without costs involved.

- *Professional web*. Professional, multidisciplinary databases are usually subscription-based. They may be accessed through a browser interface. Some well-known professional databases include: Lexis-Nexis[31] for legal matters, news, public records and business information, ISI Web of Knowledge[32] or Questel Orbit[33] for intellectual property.

- *Vanishing web*. The vanishing web describes web pages that are temporarily unavailable (e.g. when the server is down) or simply do not exist any longer.

Another type of information that falls into the category of the deep web is information that is dynamically changing. Examples include:

- news;
- job postings;
- available airline flights and last-minute hotel deals;
- stock exchange figures.

Information that is likely to be stored in a database is a part of the deep web. This can include large listings of items with a common theme. All directories are part of the deep web. Examples include:

- telephone directories;
- 'people finders' such as lists of professionals, e.g. doctors or lawyers;
- patents;
- laws;
- dictionary definitions;
- items for sale in a web store or on web-based auctions;
- digital exhibits;
- multimedia and graphical files.

Sources with deep web content may be searched and located in subject directories and search engines. There are also websites that specialise in collecting links to databases that are available on the Web. Below are listed a few examples:

- *Complete Planet*.[34] Complete Planet offers searchable access to thousands of databases for results that include summaries from the retrieved site.

- *Invisible-web.net*.[35] A directory of high quality deep web databases.

- *Direct Search*.[36] DirectSearch offers a large and growing compilation of links to search resources that contain data not easily available from the general search tools. The site is updated daily with news on search engines, news about the industry and also library news. The site is maintained by Gary Price and is a good source to keep up to date with developments.

- *Subject Directory of Search Engines*.[37] This is a topical listing of searchable databases on the web. The list is divided into Fields & Field Types (what fields you want to search, e.g. audio/music, date last modified), Search Logic (do you want to search with Boolean logic or not), Search Options (do you want to search with case sensitivity), Search Results (do you want results based on popularity) and Speciality Searches (newsgroups or professionally maintained directories) – a very useful list.

Further sources of deep web content will be listed in Chapter 6.

Notes

1. *http://www.searchenginewatch.com/links/major.html*
2. *http://www.google.com*
3. *http://www.alltheweb.com*
4. *http://www.yahoo.com*
5. *http://search.msn.com*
6. *http://www.lycos.com*
7. *http://www.askjeeves.com*
8. *http://search.aol.com/* (external)
9. *http://www.teoma.com*
10. *http://www.wisenut.com*
11. *http://www.inktomi.com*
12. *http://www.looksmart.com*
13. *http://dmoz.org/*
14. *http://www.overture.com/*
15. *http://www.easysearcher.com*
16. *http://www.directory.google.com*
17. *http://www.metacrawler.com*
18. *http://www.webcrawler.com*
19. *http://www.dogpile.com*
20. *http://infomine.ucr.edu*
21. *http://uk.yahoo.com*
22. *http://www.excite.com*
23. *http://www.netscape.com*

24. *http://www.lycos.com*

25. *http://www.msn.com*

26. *http://www.aol.co.uk*

27. *http://www.rdn.ac.uk*

28. *http://www.humbul.ac.uk*

29. *http://www.academicinfo.net/index.html*

30. *http://www.brightplanet.com*

31. *http://www.lexisnexis.com*

32. *http://www.isiwebofknowledge.com*

33. *http://www.questelorbit.com*

34. *http://www.completeplanet.com*

35. *http://invisible-web.net*

36. *http://www.freepint.com/gary/direct.htm*

37. *http://library.albany.edu/internet/choose.html*

5

Interpretation of results

L'embarras des richesses.
The more alternatives, the more difficult the choice.

Abbé d'Allainval

We tend to look at the World Wide Web as a whole. We tend to say 'the Web' is good or bad, but we have not yet learned to distinguish between the pages. The Web is just a means of making information, good and not so good, available to us. We have to try to learn to distinguish between the individual pages. You would never compare Jerry Cotton to William Shakespeare, but both are published in the same form – a book. However, both authors, Jerry Cotton and William Shakespeare, have their place in our world. We have enough experience to distinguish between them and most of the time the distinction is easy.

Recently, while browsing through an American edition of Michael Crichton's new techno-thriller, *Prey*, I was, however, suddenly unsure again. It was a beautifully bound book, with heavy paper and the pages were cut in the typically ragged American style. Of course, I had to have it. But does the beautiful and heavy paper, the clean typesetting and so on make it a quality book? I don't know. I only know that it makes compelling reading. This is an example of our decades-long experience with books: we can place Crichton,

Shakespeare and Cotton where they belong. The Web has resulted in a huge quantity of information – information which is, potentially, available anywhere at any time to anyone. Thanks to information and communication technologies, information is superficially easier to access. But because of the sheer amount of the available information and the ease with which information can be put on the Web, assessment of this information in terms of its accuracy, provenance and reliability has become much harder.

You cannot learn how to read *with* a book – you have to know how to read before that. Of course, once you know how to read, a book may help you to improve your reading skills and to interest you in literature and further reading, or even better in a particular subject. The book may act as a working tool, a working help. The same applies to the Web: we have to learn how to use it, we have to get enough experience so that we are capable of evaluating it and giving everything its due regard.

Recently, I overheard the following comment from a university student: 'I don't want to base all the sources for my thesis on the Internet. And I know for a fact that our teacher does not trust Internet sources.' Yet there are ways to cite Internet sources and ways to evaluate them. Above all, it must be remembered that the Internet is not a source as such – it is simply a means to deliver thousands of different sources to us. The Internet is only the transport medium for all this information. The Internet itself is not responsible for the information that one finds. The Internet can never be a source. The existence of doubtless thousands of home pages filled with incorrect information does not mean that every source on the Internet is of the same quality. It is therefore of the utmost importance that we use the possibilities of evaluation for every home page.

The tips that follow are especially useful if you are looking for academic, scientific or reliable information. Perhaps you are doing a search because you need information or facts for a paper you are writing or because you have a reference desk in your library and are helping students to use the Internet.

Not all web pages need to be evaluated. There is certainly no need for you to apply the checklist below for an Internet site with the official cinema listings in your region. The information on this page is as accurate as it is in the local newspaper. And on the online version as well as the print version typographic errors may happen. But this cannot be helped, even if you evaluate the page first. Also, the knowledge that you have in front of you the official, online version of your local cinema is evaluation enough. There is certainly no need here to check whether the webmaster can be contacted or if the author is really who they say they are.

On the other hand, it may well be that you are evaluating web pages, including local culture pages, because you are compiling a link list for your library – in this case the tips and checklist below will be of much use.

Above all, always question what you do and the results you get! Learn to be sceptical and then learn to trust your instincts.

In this chapter, there are quite a few technical terms and I have used them because this is what they are for, but I have also tried to include an explanation in plain English.

Evaluation criteria

There are usually five classical criteria applied to evaluate a web page:

- accuracy;
- authority;
- objectivity;
- currency;
- coverage.

To these five criteria of evaluation, two of a more technical nature are usually added:

- access;
- navigation and design.

Because of the reasons outlined above, these criteria have to be assessed under difficult conditions. We do not yet have enough years of experience to feel confident and safe.

For the purposes of this book it is more useful to concentrate on how to evaluate the content of a web page. That said, the technical points are quite important and have to be considered and evaluated in order to gain a complete picture. We will look at the technical side first.

Access

Connection speed

We have come to accept that all websites can be accessed extremely fast. According to various laboratory tests and studies, most users lose interest after only 7–8 seconds. So the aim of every web-page builder has to be to make the page available in less than 10 seconds. The build-up of a page should be no more than 10 seconds. This time is based on today's standard 56k dial-up modem. The connection should be proportionally faster with a broadband connection, perhaps as little as 5 seconds. The speed of the connection basically depends on:

- infrastructure (both sides);
- size of web pages;
- amount and size of images;
- use of so-called plug-ins.

Software requirements

Here, I will not go into too many technical details. In my opinion, a web builder has to build pages appropriate for the average user. The inclusion of animation, videos and sound requiring complicated plug-ins for a page, say, containing opera and theatre programmes is simply not appropriate. The standard question in evaluating websites in terms of software requirements is: does the site require plug-ins? Depending on the browser software and plug-ins you have installed you might not need plug-ins at all, so this question is unnecessary. However, what counts here most of all is the accordance of form with content. The use of java scripts, plug-ins and other than standard communication ports should only be applied if necessary. The form should always be in accordance with the targeted market.

Security, however, is another matter. Any website offering goods for sale with online payment needs to offer good security and encryption software. The best and most-cited example of this is without doubt the online bookshop Amazon. Their shop and payment solution is exemplary, easy to use and safe. One indication whether an online transaction is safe is if the URL changes into hypertext transfer protocol secure (https), e.g. *https://www.onlinebanking.com*. I suggest that you read the relevant 'Terms of business' before you order anything online and see what they have to say about security.

Accessibility

Content

Questions to ask include the following:

- Is there a clear distinction between free content and pages that cost?
- If there are pages that cost, is a demo/trial subscription available?
- What are the conditions of use?
- Are there offers specially designed for library access?

URL

An important part of any web page is the Internet address, the URL. In order to fully understand and later to correctly evaluate a so-called URL – the unique resource locator – it is necessary to explain in detail how this system works.

A URL consists of several components. The protocol indicates which method the web browser uses to exchange data with the file server on which the document you desire resides. The protocols today recognised by most browsers are:

■ hypertext transfer protocol;

■ hypertext transfer protocol secure;

■ file transfer protocol.

Other Internet protocols include telnet and gopher.

In a URL, the protocol used should always be followed by a colon and two forward slashes: *http://*. The host name indicates the server on which the files reside. Often, this is the name of an organisation, e.g. *http://www.organisation.org*. Note that this part of a URL is not case-sensitive. Now follows the rest of the address, e.g. *http://www.organisation.org/news* or *http://www.organisation/news/archive99.html*. This is the directory path leading to the desired document. This part of the URL is case-sensitive. It is therefore important to reproduce upper-case and lower-case letters and all punctuation with the utmost accuracy.

In order to understand error messages, it is helpful to understand the nature of the URL. I am sure you have experienced the situation where, after a lot of searching, clicking on a link which appears to promise the information you were looking for only returns the error message 'Document not found'. Do not be content with this. A few simple tricks may get you what you want if you use the logical structure of a URL to your advantage.

URLs contain directory and file names and are usually given following a logical, recurrent pattern. If you recognise such a pattern, you may be able to vary it. If for example, a (made-up) URL like *http://www.some-host.org/statistics/2001/january.html* does not work, you might be lucky with another month: *http://www.some-host.org/statistics/2001/march/html*. Once you are within the site you can work from there. Sometimes, there are obvious typing errors (especially in printed material) like the (made-up) URL *http://www.a-newspaper.com/arcive/2002.html*. In this case try: *http://www.a-newspaper.com/archive/2002.html*.

Alternatively, use the hierarchical pattern to climb up in the faulty address. Start from the end of the URL and delete one part at a time. If, for example, *http://www.largegarden.co.uk/house/bathroom/towel.html* does not work, then delete towel.html and try *http://www.largegarden.co.uk/house/bathroom*, and then, if this still does not work, *http://www.largegarden.co.uk/house/* and *http://www.largegarden.co.uk*. From the home page you might be able to find the page you were originally looking for with an internal search engine.

IP addresses

An IP address is a number that identifies each sender or receiver of information that is sent across the Internet. When you request a web page or send an e-mail, the Internet protocol (part of TCP/IP) includes your IP address in the message and sends it to the IP address you requested or to the e-mail address you are sending a note to. At the other end, the recipient can see your IP address or the e-mail sender and can respond by sending another message using the IP address it received. To make things easier for us, the IP address is usually automatically translated into the domain name or an e-mail address.

Who owns a particular IP address can be discovered through dedicated databases. The IP addresses are assigned in a delegated manner. Users are assigned IP addresses by so-called Internet service providers (ISPs). These providers obtain allocations of IP addresses from a local Internet registry (LIR), a national Internet registry (NIR), or (to make things even more complicated) from their appropriate regional Internet registry (RIR).

The owner of a website need not be identical to the hosting company (ISP). A small word of caution is advisable here: websites with illegal, offensive or insulting content or pages simply containing trash are often hiding in the relative security of huge providers such as AOL or Geocities. This raises the interesting question whether a professional hosting company shares responsibility for the content of the websites that it hosts. Large hosting companies do not actively check the content of the sites they host. They only react if their attention is drawn to pages that do not correspond to their 'Terms of business'. If you come across a site with offending content, report it immediately to the provider.

Usually, only companies with a leased connection have their own IP addresses. Because of the limited amount of available IP addresses, most other users will be assigned a temporary IP address from a pool of IP addresses owned by the Internet service provider.

You can look up who is behind an Internet address yourself on the following:

- *RIPE* (*http://ripe.net*). The RIPE Network Coordination Center manages the addresses for Europe, the Middle East, Central Asia and African countries located north of the equator.

- *APNIC* (*http://www.apnic.net*). The APNIC Asia Pacific Network Information Centre looks after addresses for the Asia and Pacific Region.

- *ARIN* (*http://www.arin.net*). ARIN, the American Registry for Internet Numbers, covers the Americas and Sub-Sahara Africa.

- *LACNIC* (*http://lacnic.net*). LACNIC, the Regional Latin-American and Caribbean ID Address Registry, manages addresses for Latin America and some Caribbean Islands.

- *SWITCH* (*http://www.switch.ch*). The Swiss Education and Research Network maintains a gateway to the above registries on its website.

I did a search on Switch on 24 March 2003 for *swisscancer.ch*, the Internet address of the organisation I once worked with. This is the result:

Domain name:	swisscancer.ch
Holder of domain name:	Swiss Cancer League,
	Jeanne Froidevaux-Mueller,
	Effingerstrasse 40, CH-3001
	Bern, Switzerland
	froidevaux@swisscancer.ch

Technical contact:	Schweizerische Krebsliga
	Ueli Wittwer
	Effingerstrasse 40-80,
	CH-3001 Bern, Switzerland
	wittwer@swisscancer.ch
Name servers:	ns1.ip-plus.net
	Ns1.swisscancer.ch
	(194.209.144.11)
Date of last registration:	26.09.1996
Date of last modification:	13.08.2001

Even this information obviously has to be regarded with caution: I do not work there anymore! In fact, I left the Swiss Cancer League at the end of October 2002. This means that this record had already been obsolete for five months at the time of writing. The problem here is that it is impossible to find out whether the Cancer League did not report the change or whether they did but Switch has been slow to update its records.

Domain names

Domain names are similar to IP addresses but there are more organisations involved in the registration and administrative process.

Top-level domains

There are two types of top-level domains, so-called generic top-level domains and country code domains. Generic domains were created for use by the Internet public, while country code domains were created to be used by individual countries as they deemed necessary. Below you will find more information about each type of top-level domain.

Country code domains

Examples of country code domains are:

- .ac   Ascension Island;
- .ad   Andorra;
- .zm   Zambia;
- .zw   Zimbabwe;
- .de   Germany;
- .jp   Japan;
- .uk   United Kingdom;
- .ch   Switzerland.

The complete country code domain list can be found on the website of the Internet Assigned Numbers Authority (IANA).[1]

Generic domains

The Internet's domain-name system (DNS) allows users to refer to websites and other resources using easier-to-remember domain names (such as 'www.icann.org') rather than the all-numeric IP addresses (such as '192.0.34.65') assigned to each computer on the Internet. Each domain name is made up of a series of character strings (called 'labels') separated by dots. The right-most label in a domain name is referred to as its 'top-level domain' (TLD), e.g. the *.com* in *http://www.tesco.com.*

The DNS forms a tree-like hierarchy. Each top-level domain includes many second-level domains (such as 'icann' in 'www .icann.org'); each second-level domain can include a number of third-level domains ('www' in 'www.icann.org').

The responsibility for operating each top-level domain (including maintaining a registry of the second-level domains within the top-level domain) is delegated to a particular organisation. These organisations are usually called 'registry operators', sometimes 'sponsors', or simply 'delegees'.

There are several types of top-level domains within the DNS:

- Top-level domains with two letters (such as .de, .mx and .jp) have been established for over 240 countries and are referred to as country code top-level domains.

- Most top-level domains with three or more characters (such as .com or .edu) are referred to as generic top-level domains.

In the 1980s, the first seven generic top-level domains were created. They were: .com, .edu, .gov, .int, .mil, .net and .org. Domain names may be registered in three of these (.com, .net and .org) without restriction; the other four have limited purposes.

Over the next 12 years, various discussions occurred concerning additional generic top-level domains, leading to the selection in November 2000 of seven new ones. These were introduced in 2001 and 2002.

In January 2003, the following generic domain codes or top-level domains were available:

Top level domain	Introduced	Purpose
.aero	2001	Reserved for members of the air-transport industry
.biz	2001	Restricted to businesses
.com	1995	Unrestricted (but intended for commercial registrants)
.coop	2001	Reserved for cooperatives
.edu	1995	United States degree-granting educational institutions of higher education
.gov	1995	Reserved exclusively for the United States government
.info	2001	Unrestricted use
.int	1998	Used only for organisations established by international treaties between governments
.mil	1995	Reserved exclusively for the United States military
.museum	2001	Reserved for museums
.name	2001	For registration by individuals
.net	1995	Unrestricted (but intended for network providers and similar organisations)
.org	1995	Unrestricted (but intended for organisations that do not fit elsewhere)
.pro	2002	This top-level domain will be restricted to credentialled accountants, lawyers, physicians and other professionals

Additional information on generic domains may be obtained from IANA.

Navigation and design

Navigation

The navigation on a web page is there to guide you, to help you get around a page. It should deliver answers to the following questions:

- Where am I?
- What can I find here?
- How do I get out of this page?
- Who can help me?

Navigation should always be appropriate to the market for which it was designed. It should also be intuitive and consistent. Elements of navigation should preferably be hierarchical and easily identifiable. They should have clear functions, should build up fast and should be available on every page.

Some links should be permanent and available on every page, for example:

- Search;
- Contact;
- Help.

Search and Help:

- Is a search possible within the site?
- Are the search criteria of the internal search engine and the relevance ranking explained?
- Is there a navigational structure, e.g. a site map?
- Is it possible to contact the webmaster on every page?

Also check whether (excessive) scrolling is necessary. With vertical scrolling the first page of the screen gets the most attention (most of the time the only attention). If horizontal scrolling is necessary, this can indicate a design error or maybe just carelessness. I would consider horizontal scrolling only a negative point in evaluation if it is a professional site.

Design

The design of a website includes:

- font;
- background;
- images;
- animations.

Design is always a matter of taste, but in my opinion there are a few things that should always be avoided. If the exact information you are looking for happens to be available on a horribly designed page, say with pink pigs as a background, then by all means ignore the background and take the information! But beware: content and form can and do differ. The layout and graphics of a website on their own are not a sufficient basis for an evaluation base an evaluation upon. A basic, perhaps not very attractive, site may well be maintained by a university department and contain very reliable and scientifically sound resources. On the other hand, the website of a seedy backyard garage may look like the site of a big international company.

Regarding design, ask yourself the following questions:

- Was the web page designed in order to appeal to the market it is aiming at?
- Does it have a professional feeling?
- Does it lead the user visually?

There are some generally accepted standards in web design which should be followed. For example, there is an internationally accepted standard that links to another page are underlined and in blue. If you are a frequent user, you get used to this. It is then very irritating if you suddenly find yourself on a page where hyperlinks to other web pages are alternating between yellow and black and are not underlined.

Font

Regarding font, you might ask yourself the following questions:

- Are standard fonts used?
- Is the size of the font a bit bigger than in printed documents?

Background

Regarding background, the following questions might be appropriate:

- Are there few colours?
- Is there no contrast?
- Does the page seem to be a patchwork instead of a whole picture?

Images

If you look at the images on a web page, ask the following:

- Are pictures and images used in a way that seems to make sense?
- Do they complement the text and the navigation or have they just been put in for decoration?
- Is there an alternative text? (This is helpful if the pictures, for some reason, do not load. The text gives you an idea of what the picture would be.)

Animation

Animation uses up a lot of resources, so ask yourself whether it is really necessary. More important, perhaps, is the correspondence between content and form.

Interaction

- Are there e-mail addresses?
- Can the webmaster be contacted?
- Are there standard feedback forms?
- Are these forms well-designed?
- What about encryption of sensitive data?

Accuracy

According to the dictionary, accurate means: 'free from error, especially as the result of care; conforming precisely to truth or a measurable standard'. It comes from the Latin *accuratus* meaning 'done carefully'. Accuracy or the verifiability of details is a very important part of any evaluation process. It is especially important if you are evaluating the work of an author unfamiliar to you or a document written by an unfamiliar organisation. Here again, the evaluation process is made more difficult because we do not yet have enough experience in dealing with online resources and it is easy for anyone to publish on the Internet. Establishing the accuracy of information tells us whether the author has integrity, is reliable and is trying to tell the truth.

You may ask yourself the following questions and apply the following criteria in order to ascertain the accuracy of a web page:

- Does the content seem to be carefully researched?
- Does the content contain obvious mistakes?
- Is the information written in a clear and comprehensible language?
- Is there an editor?
- Is there someone who seems to be responsible for the content?
- Is there a disclaimer?
- Is there a copyright notice?
- Are there any indications of the sources used?
- Are there references that seem doubtful?
- Is an explanation given of the research methods used to gather and interpret data? (This is especially important with research documents.)
- Is the methodology outlined appropriate to the topic?

- Does it allow the study to be duplicated for purposes of verification? (Again, this is of particular importance with research documents.)
- Are sources listed in a bibliography?
- Are there any hyperlinks to the sources mentioned?
- Can the background information used also be verified for accuracy?

Authority

According to the dictionary, authority means: 'the power to issue directives accompanied by the right to expect obedience; the position of a person who has such a power; delegated power or authorisation'.

Evaluation of authority is made difficult if you are searching for a subject that you are not familiar with. Authorship is perhaps the major criterion used in evaluating information.

Questions to ask regarding the authority of a web page are as follows:

- Who is the author? Who wrote this?
- Is it a personal page or site?
- Is the author a qualified, recognised and trustworthy expert in his or her field?
- Is the author a well-known and well-regarded name you recognise?

When you find an author you do not recognise, ask yourself the following questions:

- Is the author mentioned in a positive fashion by another author or another person you trust as an authority?

- Did you find or link to the author's web document from another document you trust?

- Does the web/Internet document you are reading give biographical information, including the author's position, institutional affiliation and address?

- Is biographical information available by linking to another document? This might enable you to judge whether the author's credentials allow him/her to speak with authority on a given topic.

- Can the author be contacted for further information?

- Is there an address and telephone number as well as an e-mail address for the author in order to request further information on his or her work and professional background? An e-mail address alone is not enough!

- Is the author a member of any institutions?

- Is there a masthead that gives information on the intellectual property situation and publishing policy?

Further checks on the authority of an author may be made via any references given or through online reviews.

When we look for information with some type of critical value, we want to know the basis of the authority with which the author speaks. In the world of books and printed material, usually the author's manuscript has undergone editing in order to verify that it meets the standards or the aims of the organisation or publishing house. This may, of course, include peer review. On the Internet, ask the following questions to assess the role and authority of the 'publisher', which in this case means the server (computer) where the document resides:

- Is the name of an organisation given on the document you are reading?

- Are there headers, footers or a distinctive watermark that show the document to be part of an official academic or scholarly website?

- Can you contact the webmaster from this document?

- If not, is there a hyperlink to a page where such information is listed?

- Is this organisation recognised in the field in which you are searching?

- Is this organisation suitable to address the topic at hand?

- Can you ascertain the relationship of the author and the publisher/server?

- Was the document that you are viewing prepared as part of the author's professional duties (and, by extension, within his/her area of expertise)?

- Or is the relationship of a casual or for-fee nature, telling you nothing about the author's credentials within an institution?

It is very important to check the domain registration of a website. Ask yourself:

- Can you verify the identity of the server where the document resides?

- Does this web page actually reside in an individual's personal Internet account, rather than being part of an official website?

If you want to find out the owner of a domain name, you can use a free-of-charge domain name search directory, e.g. Checkdomain (*http://www.checkdomain.com*) or NetNames (*http://www.netnames.co.uk/dnrs/netnames.client.login*). The NetNames database gives detailed information on any registered domain name.

If you find that the web page is in fact residing in an individual's personal Internet account, then perhaps this type of information resource should be approached with some caution.

Objectivity

According to the dictionary, objectivity means: 'to be concerned with or expressing the nature of external reality rather than personal feelings or beliefs; dealing with facts without distortion by personal feelings or prejudices; belonging to the external world and observable or verifiable'.

You might be able to ascertain the objectivity of a web page by asking the following questions:

- Is the available information unbiased and objective?
- Does the information seem to lean towards an opinion? Does it seem to be there to influence the opinion of the reader?
- Are the aims and purposes of the authors obvious?
- Is there any publicity on the page?
- If yes, is it clearly separated from content?
- Are there advertising banners?

- Are these clearly separated from the content, at least visually?

- Are product or company names used?

- Are there any links to commercial sites?

- Are sponsors clearly marked as such?

- What are the aims of the authors?

- Does the author want to convey neutral information or manipulate the site visitor?

- Does the document reside on the web server of an organisation that has a clear interest in the issue at hand?

- Does the document reside on the web server of an organisation that has a political or philosophical agenda?

- Is an extremist point of view hidden behind an educational front?

Information is rarely neutral. Because data is used in selective ways to form information, it often represents a point of view. Every writer wants to prove his point, and will use the data and information that assists him in doing so. When evaluating information found on the Web, it is important to examine *who* is providing the information you are viewing, and what might be their *point of view* or *bias*. The popularity of the Internet makes it the perfect venue for commercial and socio-political publishing. These areas in particular are open to highly 'interpretative' uses of data. It may be helpful to remember the following points:

- If you are looking at a company website, assume that the information published there on the company itself will probably present it in the most positive light.

- If you are looking at products produced and sold by a company – even if published on their website and presented in a professional manner – it is still an advertisement.

- If you are looking at material published about a political figure on the website of another political party, you are reading what the opposition says.

- Would you go to a political or religious organisation to provide you with scientific information on human genetics?

Many areas of research and inquiry deal with controversial questions, and often the more controversial an issue is, the more interesting it is. When looking for information, it is *always* critical to remember that everyone has an opinion. Because the structure of the Internet allows for easy self-publication, the variety of points of view and bias will be the widest possible.

Currency

According to the dictionary, currency means: 'general use, acceptance, or prevalence, or the state of being in general use; in vogue; occurring in or belonging to the present time'. It comes from the Latin *currere*, 'to run'.

In web evaluating terms, it refers to the timeliness of information. For most types of document, currency is rather important, as is the regularity with which the data is updated. Missing dates not only mean that the document probably has not been updated recently; it can also be an indication that it was not written by professionals. Beware of the automatic date – this is just an element of information: it is not an indicator of currency. Updating on a regular basis applies only to documents where there is a need to add data or update it on a constant basis.

Ask yourself the following questions to ascertain currency:

- Is the page dated?
- Does the document include the date(s) at which the information was gathered?
- Does the document refer to clearly dated information?
- Is the date just an automatic date?
- Does the content give a current impression?
- Is there a publication date?
- What is the date of the last update? Are the hyperlinks current?
- Do they still link to current sites or are there many broken links?
- Does it seem to be updated on a regular basis?

Coverage

According to the dictionary, coverage means: 'an area or amount covered; inclusion within the scope of discussion or reporting'. It also means the number or percentage of people reached by a communication medium. The coverage of a website may give you an indication of the context in which the author situates his or her work. This reveals what the author knows about his or her discipline and its practices, allowing you to evaluate the author's scholarship or knowledge of trends in the area under discussion. Questions to ask regarding the coverage of a website are:

- Which subject is covered?
- In what depth is it covered?
- What does the document say?
- Is it written in a clear language?
- Are the documents well-structured?
- Are all documents written in the same language and tone?
- Does the site give the impression of being put together randomly and incompletely?
- Does it contain many typing or spelling mistakes?
- Are the essential subjects being covered comprehensively or just superficially?
- Is there exclusivity?
- Is the subject covered elsewhere?
- Is there information on the page that cannot be found elsewhere?
- Does the document include a bibliography?
- Does the author allude to or display knowledge of related sources, with proper attribution?
- Does the author display knowledge of theories, schools of thought or techniques usually considered appropriate in the treatment of his or her subject?
- If the author is using a new theory or technique as a basis for research, does he or she discuss the value and/or limitations of this new approach?

■ If the author's treatment of the subject is controversial, is this acknowledged by the author?

Another component of the coverage is the links offered on a page. A well-maintained link list is a good addition to a subject already well covered. However, the best link list is of no use if it is not well-maintained. Therefore, ask yourself the following questions:

■ Are there many dead links on the page?

■ Are the links to external sites clearly marked?

■ Is there a disclaimer?

A good example of clearly marked links to external sites with a corresponding disclaimer is found on the site of the American Cancer Society:[2]

> You are about to leave the American Cancer Society website. Clicking the link below or 'Continue' at the bottom of this page will take you to a website to which our Privacy Policy does not apply. Links are provided as a public service and for informational purposes only. No endorsement is made or implied.

I think there is nothing more frustrating than finding a comprehensive link list on the subject that you are researching and finding that every second link is dead. A link list with many dead links is an indication that the list is not looked after properly. Dead links within a website are often caused by inconsistent navigation. Dead links that link (or rather do not link) to external sites are usually caused because the page linked to has moved or does not exist anymore. If I chance upon such an ill-maintained list, this always leaves a bad impression. Why? Because it obviously is not important enough for the people who maintain the page to check the links they offer regularly. If the company or the person is not willing to maintain the link list then they should not offer one in the first place.

A link list should be checked on a regular basis. There are two ways to do this. Depending on the size of the list it can be done manually. The other possibility is to install software that does the job for you. However, such updating software only checks whether the hyperlink to the other site is still working – it will not check whether the content of the site is still the same.

For example, the CDNow website *http://www.cdnow.com* used to be an independent and comprehensive online shop for music CDs and DVDs. Now, if you type in the address, you are automatically redirected to Amazon at *http://www.amazon .com*. For checking this, and also as a good source to see how design has developed over the years, go to the Wayback Machine at *http://www.archive.org* and type in the Internet address you are interested in. The Wayback Machine is a digital Internet archive and the aim is to store at least some of the many websites in order to preserve at least parts of the Web.

Checklists

The examples of checklists provided below may be used as a support and guidelines for your own evaluation of web pages. Bear in mind that evaluation is hardly ever easy and with some documents a lot of instinct and experience will be necessary to judge them correctly. Ask yourself: who is talking about what to whom? This journalistic standard formula helps when you are evaluating web pages.

I have provided two different examples. But first, let us start with some general tips.

General tips

- Always start the evaluation of a web page on the homepage.
- Always evaluate external links separately.
- Always evaluate parts of frames separately if they belong to different sites.
- Make sure to note the URL correctly.
- An evaluation is always only a picture of the moment.
- And it is evaluated by a human being who is therefore susceptible to subjective impressions.
- It is recommended that you re-evaluate web pages on a regular basis.
- It is possible to emphasise the pages of a site differently.
- Always use criteria oriented towards your market, so if you are evaluating a web page aimed at the young, put more emphasis on the use of graphics.
- Use the technical conditions of the main market group as standard, if known.
- It might be useful to divide further into Need to/Nice to/Should to.
- Revisit pages: they change!
- An evaluation is always personal, and the experiences of the person who evaluates the site are reflected in that evaluation.

Checklist 1

URL:	http://www.penguin.co.uk	Key	
Date:	9 February 2003	1	Poor
Evaluated by:	Jeanne Froidevaux	2	Many reservations
Evaluation:	Overall Impression 5	3	Some reservations
	Access 4	4	Good
	Design 5	5	Very good
	Content 5		

Access		
Criteria	*Evaluation*	*Comments*
Accessibility/connection		
Could the site be easily accessed or was it partially overloaded or not accessible after several tries?	5	Accessed on the first try
Are the pages built up fast (max. 10 seconds?)	4	Took a bit more than 10 seconds
Software requirements		
Is the form of the site corresponding to its content?	5	Yes
Accessibility of the content		
Is the site public domain (therefore free of charge), or are there parts that partially or completely cost? Are these parts clearly marked as such?		Content (database and news of available books) free of charge; ordering of books – obviously cost involved
Is a special library access being offered for the parts that cost?		Not relevant

Criteria	Evaluation	Comments
Is a registration necessary to gain access to documents? If yes, is detailed personal information required? Are they being transmitted/ encrypted?		No registration necessary
What are the conditions of use? Are there explicit restrictions?		Not relevant
Is there an archive on the site?	5	Not relevant, but all available books are online
Accessibility		
Is the site indexed in the major search engines?	5	Yes
Is the URL simple and meaningful?	5	Couldn't be more simple or meaningful. It's also logical
Has the URL recently been changed?	5	No indication, no re-direct
Design and navigation		
Navigation		
Does the design, navigation and presentation make a professional impression?	5	Yes. It is consistent with their book covers
Are the navigational elements clearly recognisable as such and incorporated into the design in a consistent manner?	5	Yes. On the left side and across the page, horizontally on top
Is this so on every page?	5	Yes
Is the navigation appropriate for the targeted market and the content?	5	Yes, perhaps too much information on a page, rather small font, but target market are people who are used to reading, so therefore no problem

Criteria	Evaluation	Comments
Is the navigation complicated and mysterious, or is it intuitively easy to navigate?	5	Clear and easy
Is the content divided into manageable units or is excessive scrolling (horizontally as well as vertically) necessary?	4	Scrolling necessary horizontally, but not in excess. Considering the vast amount of available information this is justified, otherwise there would be too many clicks necessary to get to a page. The page for children has less text and more funny pictures
Are there hyperlinks between documents?	5	Yes
Are the central navigational elements like Home, Help, Search and shopping basket accessible from every page within the site?	5	Basket, Account, Home, Search and main navigation on every page
Is there an easily accessible and well-functioning search capability?	5	Search possible for title, author or ISBN. When no results, it is possible to do an advanced search
Is there a comprehensive search tool included?	5	Yes. The advanced search allows searching with key word, published date and the media format (cassette, game, paperback)
Design		
Is the design target-group oriented? Does it make a professional impression?	5	Yes
Is the use of animations and visual elements useful and suitable or irritating?	5	Yes, it's useful

Criteria	Evaluation	Comments
Are type and size of fonts (if not standard) readable?	4	Yes
Does the background help or hinder the readability?	5	Mostly white
Are hyperlinks displayed in standard format?	4	No, some links are pictures, some hypertext links are not blue, but everything is consistent with the main design
Is there an alternative text for images?		
Links		
Are there any links (internal or external) that are dead?	5	Didn't find any
Are links to external sites clearly marked as such?	5	There is no message announcing the external site, but a new browser window opens
Do the links to external sites seem trustworthy?		
Interaction		
Are interaction possibilities like e-mail and feedback forms used in an effective manner?		
Are there contact details?	5	Under the heading 'Contact us' there is a comprehensive list of contact details, listing all the relevant persons with telephone numbers and e-mail addresses

Content		
Criteria	*Evaluation*	*Comments*
Authority		
Who exactly is the author of the pages? Are name, address, telephone, fax, e-mail, membership of institutions given? Is it a personal site or page?	5	Penguin, the organisation, is the author. All contact details given
Is there any information on the qualifications of the author?		Not relevant
Is the author (well) known/trustworthy?		
Is there a connection between author and Internet address?		
May the author be contacted?		
Is it possible to check the information given through other sources?		
Are sources given? If yes, are they known/trustworthy?		
Is there a masthead which gives information about aim, authors, target market, policies, etc.?		
Coverage		
Which subjects are being treated?	5	Information on all their books
What claim is made regarding depth and comprehensiveness of the topic?		

Criteria	Evaluation	Comments
Is the page unique? Are original articles published?		
Accuracy		
Does the content make a carefully researched impression? Does it contain obvious mistakes? Is it written in a clear and understandable language?	5	Carefully written and presented
Are there any indications that the content has been checked through a higher authority?		Not relevant
Is there a disclaimer? Is it phrased in a clear way?		
Is there a copyright notice for the site and its content?	5	Yes, Copyright Notice, Terms and Conditions, Privacy Policy
Currency		
Does the content make a current impression (dates, persons, information)?	5	Yes
Is there a publication date?	5	There are publication dates for every book
Does every document have a publication date? Does it say the date when it was last updated?	3	There is the daily date. The list 'New this month' (February 2003) contained the latest book dated January 2003, and the oldest book with a publication date August 2000
Objectivity		
Is the information given in a neutral way or is it written to manipulate/influence the opinion of the reader?	5	Yes of course, but it is publicity for their books

Criteria	Evaluation	Comments
Are the aims of the author/ the authors/the page clearly stated?		
Is there publicity? If yes, is it clearly separated from content?		
Is there any indication of sponsors? If yes, how are they visible?		
Personal impression		
What is your personal and subjective impression, your gut-feeling, of the evaluated page?	5	Highly professional, rich, clearly arranged site, a joy to browse. Perhaps a bit slow. This evaluation was made with a broadband 256 kb connection)

Checklist 2

URL:	*http://www.annoyances.org*	Key		
Date:	26 March 2003	1	Poor	
Evaluated by:	Jeanne Froidevaux	2	Many reservations	
Evaluation:	Overall Impression	2	3	Some reservations
	Access	5	4	Good
	Design	3	5	Very good
	Content	2		

Access

Criteria	*Evaluation*	*Comments*
Accessibility/connection		
Could the site be easily accessed or was it partially overloaded or not accessible after several tries?	5	Worked on the first try on 17 March, and again without problems on 22 and 26 March
Are the pages built up fast (max. 10 seconds?)	5	Yes
Software requirements		
Is the form of the site corresponding to its content?	5	Yes. Simple text and information, not overloaded
Accessibility of the content		
Is the site public domain (therefore free of charge), or are there parts that partially or completely cost? Are these parts clearly marked as such?		It is public domain. There is a copyright notice saying 'Please do not plagiarise; redistributing these pages without permission is strictly prohibited'
Is a special library access being offered for the parts that cost?		Not relevant

Criteria	Evaluation	Comments
Is a registration necessary to gain access to documents? If yes, is detailed personal information required? Are they being transmitted encrypted?		Not relevant
What are the conditions of use? Are there explicit restrictions?		Not relevant
Is there an archive on the site?	5	Not an archive as such, but all articles are available and categorised into subject and also searchable
Accessibility		
Is the site indexed in the major search engines?	5	Yes
Is the URL simple and meaningful?	2	Simple yes, meaningful I don't know. (To my mind, rather annoying)
Has the URL recently been changed?	5	No
Design and navigation		
Navigation		
Do the design, the navigation and the presentation make a professional impression?	4	Yes, it is very streamlined. Personal remark: why do professionals have to be so negative?)
Are the navigational elements clearly recognisable as such and incorporated into the design in a consistent manner?	5	Yes, on the left and across the top
Is this so on every page?	5	Yes

Criteria	Evaluation	Comments
Is the navigation appropriate for the targeted market and the content?	5	Yes, perhaps a bit much information on a page, rather small font, but target market are people who are used to reading, so therefore no problem
Is the navigation complicated and mysterious, or is it intuitively easy to navigate?	5	Clear and easy
Is the content divided into manageable units or is excessive scrolling (horizontally as well as vertically) necessary?	4	Yes. Some vertical scrolling necessary, but here it is definitely the content that counts
Are there hyperlinks between documents?	5	Yes
Are the central navigational elements like Home, Help, Search and shopping basket accessible from every page within the site?	5	Yes. They are Search, Help and Home
Is there an easily accessible and well-functioning search capability?	5	Yes. It is in the horizontal navigation on every page
Is there a comprehensive search tool included?		Yes. It is possible to enter one or more keywords. It is also possible to use the Articles and Discussion Forum areas to locate solutions. Boolean terms can be chosen from a list, words of fewer than two letters and very common words such as *the* and *it* are not indexed

Criteria	Evaluation	Comments
Design		
Is the design target-group oriented? Does it make a professional impression?		Yes
Is the use of animations and visual elements useful and suitable or irritating?	5	Bare minimum, but this makes good sense on a page like this
Are type and size of fonts (if not standard) readable?	4	Yes, they are dark grey on white
Does the background help or hinder the readability?	4	Helps. It is white and therefore neutral
Are hyperlinks displayed in standard format?	4	No, they are black instead of blue, but again, this is consistent with the overall design
Is there an alternative text for images?		Yes, but there are only one or two images on the whole site
Links		
Are there any links (internal or external) that are dead?	5	None that I tested
Are links to external sites clearly marked as such?	5	There is no message announcing the external site, but a new browser window opens
Do the links to external sites seem trustworthy?	5	Yes, they are all links to online book shops where it is possible to buy the books by the author of the site

Criteria	Evaluation	Comments
Interaction		
Are interaction possibilities like e-mail and feedback forms used in an effective manner?	2	There is a *Report a Broken Link* and a *Contact form*. The *Report a Broken Link* can be found under *Help* and there under the heading of *I ran into a problem with this website*), the *Contact Form* can be found under *Help* and there under *I want to learn more about annoyances.org*, the form is then at the bottom of the page, which involves scrolling. Personally, I would not search for a contact form under the heading of help
Are there contact details?	5	Under the heading 'Contact us' is a comprehensive list of contact details, listing all the relevant persons with telephone numbers and e-mail addresses
Content		
Authority		
Who exactly is the author of the pages? Are name, address, telephone, fax, e-mail, membership of institutions given? Is it a personal site or page?	1	Nothing specific or personal on the author. There is a mission statement on the site, where one finds that a certain David A. Karp is the author
Is there any information on the qualifications of the author?	5	Under the section *Recognitions and Awards*
Is the author (well) known/trustworthy?		The author obviously writes books for O'Reilly publishers

Criteria	Evaluation	Comments
Is there a connection between author and Internet address?		No
May the author be contacted?	2	Not directly
Is it possible to check the information given through other sources?		Yes, for example directly with Microsoft
Are sources given? If yes, are they known/trustworthy?		
Is there a masthead which gives information about aim, authors, target market, policies, etc.?	3	Not as such, but there is the mission statement, and the connection to O'Reilly publishers (Further research shows that O'Reilly publishes mainly books about Unix)
Coverage		
Which subjects are being treated?		Problems, bugs and their solutions for Windows XP, Windows ME, Windows 2000, Windows 98 and Windows 95
What claim is made regarding depth and comprehensiveness of the topic?	3	No claim is made. The treatment of the problems does not go deep enough, according to a specialist I asked. Some articles do not even treat software bugs and problems but only small things that the author is annoyed about
Is the page unique? Are original articles published?		

Criteria	Evaluation	Comments
Accuracy		
Does the content make a carefully researched impression? Does it contain obvious mistakes? Is it written in a clear and understandable language?	2	Yes. Clear if not objective. The solutions to the problems do not go very deep and some problems are not really problems at all, just facts. Some problems are just outlined, but no useable and useful solution is given
Are there any indications that the content has been checked through a higher authority?		No
Is there a disclaimer? Is it phrased in a clear way?		
Is there a copyright notice for the site and its content?	5	Copyright notice: 'Please do not plagiarise; redistributing these pages without permission is strictly prohibited'
Currency		
Does the content make a current impression (dates, persons, information)?	4	Yes. There is a daily date, most certainly automatically generated. The articles contain a 'last updated' date
Is there a publication date?		
Does every document have a publication date? Does it say the date when it was last updated?	5	Yes. Every article has a 'last updated' date

Criteria	Evaluation	Comments
Objectivity		
Is the information given in a neutral way or is it written to manipulate/influence the opinion of the reader?	1	No, it is not given in a neutral way. There is a clear antipathy against Microsoft, and the tone is sometimes quite aggressive
Are the aims of the author/the authors/the page clearly stated?	5	Yes
Is there publicity? If yes, is it clearly separated from content?		
Is there any indication of sponsors? If yes, how are they visible?		
Personal impression		
What is your personal and subjective impression, your gut-feeling, of the evaluated page?	2	First, this makes a very professional impression. This impression does not last, however. The professionalism is marred through the aggressive and subjective tone

Notes

1. *http://www.iana.org*
2. *http://www.cancer.org*

6

Teaching customers what you know and knowing what your customers want

It is our first duty to serve society, and, after we have done that, we may attend wholly to the salvation of our own souls. A youthful passion for abstracted devotion should not be encouraged.

Samuel Johnson, 1709–84

Any information is useless to the average consumer unless it is selectively filtered through appropriate channels and gatekeepers, and translated into comprehensible language. We as librarians have the opportunity to be these filters, these gatekeepers.

According to a report published by the OECD,[1] the Organisation for Economic Cooperation and Development, there is a wide variation in literacy levels even among technologically advanced countries. Obviously, in all countries surveyed, a large number of adults lack the skills needed for coping with the demands of everyday life and work in our complex, advanced society.

The Internet is just another, albeit a very powerful, tool to find information on any subject. Like any tool it must be used with care and professional knowledge. Anyone can be encouraged to do their own research on the Web. However, I think that it is the role and duty of information professionals to lead our customers towards reliable information. We have various means to promote and recommend comprehensive and accurate websites but we cannot forbid or ban websites with dubious or illegal content. However, if we are responsible for our library's website, we can offer our expertise by compiling link lists with reliable websites. We can offer tutorials and courses in Internet searching for library visitors. We can offer checklists on how to judge and evaluate websites. We can train people to compare the form of a website with its content. We can educate our customers and clients about the variability in completeness and accuracy.

Of course, to achieve all this, to be able to recommend good websites to others and to be trusted by them means that we always have to be one step ahead of them. We have to keep abreast of new developments and innovations in information provision and to exploit these to the full advantage of all involved. To achieve this confidence and professionalism, we have to regularly attend training courses and lectures; we have to read relevant books and articles. I believe that constant and appropriate training will lead us to professionalism and this professionalism, if passed on to others, will lead to trust in return.

But most importantly, we have to constantly use the Internet, or rather the Web, ourselves. Practise and play with it every day! A good way to do this is to do some browsing or surfing. Take the time to browse the Internet regularly, if only for 15 minutes a week. Pick a subject you are interested in, either because it is your hobby or because you have a professional interest. Albert Einstein said: 'You learn the most, when you like to do something so much that you do not even notice how time flies.'[2]

It is our duty as information professionals and librarians serving a community to offer various sources of information and to guide our customers to these sources. We are here to provide effective access to information resources to support teaching, learning and research.

> **Example**
>
> Recently we had a student in the library searching for biographical information on the author Liza Dalby. Her latest book had only just been published in German, and there was, predictably, no information on her in *Kindlers Literaturlexikon* (a German biographical index on authors). I asked the student whether he had tried the Web. He had, and he had not found anything. So, of course, I promised to look into it for him. My colleague got the book and I did a search. I had never heard of Liza Dalby before myself. I simply typed 'liza dalby' in Google and got the following results: I found her personal homepage, *http://www.lizadalby.com* and her main website, *http://www.taleofmurasaki.com*.

Maintaining a link list on your public Internet station

Another possibility to offer your customers is the knowledge that you have – to offer them an edited link list on your public Internet station. I am aware of the changing nature of Internet sites and the somewhat contradictory undertaking of publishing Internet addresses in a book. The Internet resources mentioned in this chapter, and throughout the book, are simply an example. They should encourage you to discover Internet addresses for yourself and to develop your own list as you go along. Here I have put the focus on free online services.

Let us assume that your library uses the Dewey classification system, so it would only be natural to maintain a list using the same system. So the main folders in your web browser would perhaps look like this:

000 Computers, Information and General Reference

100 Philosophy and Psychology

200 Religion, Theology and Mythology

300 Social Sciences, Law, Administration and Government

400 Languages

500 Natural Sciences and Mathematics

600 Applied Science and Medicine

700 Fine Arts and Recreation

800 Literature, Rhetoric and Criticism

900 Geography and History

If you maintain your link list with the Dewey Decimal Classification (DDC), then it is essential that your library obtains the proper copyright permission from OCLC Online Computer Library Center, Inc.[3] The following list is, as ever, not nearly complete or representative, but it should serve as an idea and perhaps you might use these links and (my personal) annotations as a starting point for your own list. You might also want to list any special collections that your library might have, e.g. special collections about your region.

Of course, the following Internet resources may also help you in your daily work or for doing your own research.

000 Computers, Information and General Reference

000 Computers, Internet and systems

- *IT-related dictionary Techtarget (http://whatis.techtarget .com/)*

  This online dictionary offers definitions for thousands of the most current information technology-related words (from ADSL to zip drive). The site also includes an IT crossword puzzle.

- *Cornell Computer Science Technical Report Collection (http://cs-tr.cs.cornell.edu)*

  Research papers and papers with an international focus on all aspects of computer science. Free of charge.

020 Library & information science

- *Libraryspot (http://www.libraryspot.com)*

  Contains many links to online library catalogues and other reference works. Specials: Library Site of the Month and Reference Site of the Month. Free of charge.

- *Mimas database (http://dois.mimas.ac.uk)*

  Database of articles and conference proceedings published in electronic format in the area of library and information science. Some articles are full-text.

■ *Internet Library for Librarians* (*http://itcompany.com/inforetriever/cat.htm*)

A portal designed for librarians to locate Internet resources related to their profession.

030 Encyclopaedias and books of facts

■ *Pinakes* (*http://www.hw.ac.uk/lib/WWW/irn/pinakes.html*)

Collection of various subject gateways, free of charge. This gateway is hosted by the Heriot-Watt University in Edinburgh.

■ *Xrefer* (*http://www.xrefer.com*)

Xrefer started in the year 2000 as a free-of-charge site that charged only for advertising space. They now specialise in the 'production of high-value institutional reference services'. Parts of their reference service are still free of charge and include such works as:

– *The Penguin Biographical Dictionary of Women*
– *The Oxford Companion to Philosophy*
– *A Dictionary of English Place-Names*
– *A Dictionary of Science* (Oxford University Press).

■ *Scibase* (*http://www.thescientificworld.com*)

Article database of international medical and technical literature since 1965. Articles may be ordered and paid for online; search free of charge.

■ *AcqWeb* (*http://acqweb.library.vanderbilt.edu*)

A good place for librarians and other professionals interested in acquisitions and collection development, providing links to information and resources of interest to librarians with acquisitions or collection development responsibilities. Sources for verification of bibliographic information; e-mail addresses of interest to librarians; associations and organisations of use to or for acquisitions and collection development librarians; electronic journals and newsletters of professional interest; archives for electronic conferences of professional interest; web reference resources of use to acquisitions and collection development librarians; gateways to more topical websites of interest; and links to search engines and subject classifications of the Web. International, free of charge.

050 Magazines, journals and serials

- *Newslibrary (http://www.newslibrary.com)*
Searchable archive of many American newspapers. Free of charge.
- *Internet Library of Early Journals (http://bodley.ox.ac .uk/ilej)*
English newspapers of the eighteenth and nineteenth centuries in digitalised format. Free of charge.

100 Philosophy and Psychology

100 Philosophy

- *Stanford Encyclopaedia of Philosophy (http://plato .stanford.edu)*

Started in 1995 it is constantly being developed. Free of charge.

150 Psychology

- *Psycline (http://www.psycline.org)*
  Database with psychological and social science journals; search possible for journals and articles. Free of charge.

- *Psych Web (http://www.psychwww.com)*
  Psychology-related information and links for students and teachers of psychology.

200 Religion, Theology and Mythology

- *Encyclopaedia mythica (http://www.pantheon.org)*
  Mythological subjects; definitions of gods and supernatural beings from all over the world. With image gallery and genealogical plates. Free of charge.

300 Social Sciences, Law, Administration and Government

- *SOSIG (http://www.sosig.ac.uk)*
  The Social Sciences, Business and Law hub from the Resource Discovery Network links to Internet resources on Business, Accountancy, Management, Economics, Finance, Industry and Commerce, Higher Education, Teaching Methods, Environmental Sciences and Issues,

Ethnology, Ethnography, Anthropology, European Studies, Economic and Political Geography, Government and Public Administration, Law, UK Law, Philosophy, Metaphysics, International Relations, Psychology, Social Science, Social Welfare, Social Work, Sociology, Statistics, Demography, Women's Studies and Women's History.

- *Eurostudies (http://www.sosig.ac.uk/eurostudies)*

  Database with European studies; searchable via specific countries. Free of charge.

- *Parlit (http://www.ipu.org/parlit-e)*

  Literature on structure, political systems and laws of various nations since 1992. Free of charge.

310 Statistics

- *Infonation (http://www.cyberschoolbus.un.org/infonation/info.asp)*

  Allows comparisons of statistical data between members of the UN; well-made graphics. Free of charge.

330 Economics

- *NetEc (http://Netec.wustl.edu)*

  Working papers on economy, Internet resources. Free of charge.

340 Law

- *Eurlex (http://Europa.eu.int/eur-lex)*

Law of the European Union. Free of charge.

■ *Lawlinks (http://www.ukc.ac.uk/library/lawlinks/default .htm)*

Legal information on the Internet; an annotated list of websites compiled by Sara Carter at the University of Kent.

370 Education

■ *ERIC Database (http://Askeric.org/eric)*

Largest database on educational issues, 1966 to present day. Free of charge.

400 Languages

■ *Ethnologue (http://www.ethnologue.com)*

Ethnologue is a bibliographic database on almost all languages of the world (contains *c.*1,000 languages), and on international language research. Free of charge.

500 Natural Sciences and Mathematics

500 Science

■ *Natural History Museum (http://www.nhm.ac.uk)*

This beautiful site contains many links; databases on entomology, zoology and botany. There is also a picture library, and it is free of charge.

510 Mathematics

- *Directories of Mathematics Journals (http://www.shef.ac .uk/library/elecjnls/ejmaths.html)*

  The University of Sheffield maintains a directory of mathematical journals.

- *Mathforum (http://www.mathforum.org)*

  Combined archive and portal to web resources, educational issues, help forums, mailing lists and teaching materials.

- *EEVL Internet Guide to Mathematics (http://www.eevl .ac.uk/mathematics)*

  The EEVL Mathematics Guide also links to UK and worldwide Maths Departments and Institutions.

- *Alan Turing (http://www.turing.org.uk)*

  This site is dedicated to the founder of modern computer science, Alan Turing. It is maintained by Andrew Hodges, who is also the author of Turing's biography, *Alan Turing: the Enigma.*

520 Astronomy

- *The NASA Astrophysics Data System (http://adswww .harvard.edu)*

  Databases on the following subjects: Astronomy, Astrophysics, Physics, Geophysics, Instrumentation. Free of charge.

530 Physics

- *World of Biography – Physicists (http://scienceworld.wolfram.com/biography/topics/Physicists.html)*

  Biographical information on important physicists; with bibliographic notes and pictures. Free of charge.

- *SPIRES HEP Literature Database (http://www.slac.stanford.edu/spires/hep)*

  Literature database high-energy physics since 1974; includes preprints, dissertations, reports and conference papers. Free of charge.

540 Chemistry

- *Chemfinder (http://www.chemfinder.com)*

  The Chemfinder database is searchable for chemical formulae and structures of specific elements. Free of charge.

- *Chemdex (http://www.chemdex.org)*

  Directory of chemistry, maintained by the Department of Chemistry at the University of Sheffield.

570 Biology and life sciences

- *Biology Browser (http://www.biologybrowser.org)*

  Biology Browser is a portal designed by BIOSIS to connect life sciences researchers with free, useful resources and other researchers from across the world. The site contains a discussion forum, evaluated web links and a large link list.

580 Plants (Botany)

- *Plants Database (http://plants.usda.gov)*

  Maintained by United States Department of Agriculture; incl. Plant of the Week. Free of charge.

- *The Lindley Library (http://www.rhs.org.uk/libraries _london.asp)*

  The Lindley Library is the world's foremost horticultural library, with a comprehensive collection of horticultural literature from the sixteenth century to the present day. The collection in London comprises over 50,000 books, ranging in date from 1514 to the present, over 300 current periodicals as well as many older runs of periodicals, 18,000 botanical drawings, the country's largest collection of horticultural trade catalogues and the Society's archives.

- *The Royal Horticultural Society (http://www.rhs.org.uk)*

  Databases: Plant Finder, Garden Finder, Nursery Finder, Event Finder. Links to others. Also a list of RHS studies of various plants, free of charge.

- *PSIgate (http://www.psigate.ac.uk)*

  PSIgate (Physical Sciences Information Gateway) is the physical sciences hub of the Resource Discovery Network and provides access to high-quality Internet resources for students, researchers and practitioners in the physical sciences. Subjects include:

  Astrochemistry and astrobiology, Astrophysics, Celestial mechanics, Cosmology, General astronomy, History of astronomy, Observational astronomy, Solar system,

Universe, Chemistry, Earth sciences, Physics, Science history and policy, and General science.

Each resource in the main catalogue has been selected by information professionals and subject specialists to ensure relevance and quality. A full description of each resource is provided, together with a range of other information and direct access to the resource itself.

PSIgate is also developing additional services in support of the needs of the physical sciences community, such as current awareness services (jobs, news and conferences), science reference materials, tools, the hosting of other searchable databases and other community features. Further services include a latest science news service from the Internet and also job and career resources.

600 Applied Science and Medicine

■ *Internet Guide to Engineering, Mathematics and Computing (EEVL) (http://www.eevl.ac.uk)*

EEVL is the Internet Guide to Engineering, Mathematics and Computing, and is also part of the Resource Discovery Network. EEVL's mission is to provide access to quality networked engineering, mathematics and computing resources, and to be the national focal point for online access to information in these subjects. It is an award-winning free service, created and run by a team of information specialists from a number of universities and institutions in the UK.

The gateway's target audience is students, staff and researchers in higher and further education, as well as anyone else working, studying or looking for information in Engineering, Mathematics and Computing. Subject areas include:

Aerospace & Defence Engineering, Bioengineering and Chemical Engineering in Engineering; Algebra, Analysis, Applications, Geometry, Topology, Numerical Analysis, Probability in Mathematics and Computer Applications, Computer Systems Organisation, Computing Methodologies in Computing.

The site offers a news service, called *Latest News in Engineering*, where the latest news from all over the world on Aerospace and Defence Engineering, Bioengineering, Chemical Engineering, Civil Engineering, Electrical, Electronic and Computer Engineering, Engineering Design, Manufacturing Engineering, Materials Engineering, Mechanical Engineering and Related Industries, Mining, Nanotechnology, Petroleum and Offshore Engineering is collected.

- *BIOME (http://biome.ac.uk)*

  Hub maintained by the Resource Discovery Network, offering free access via a searchable catalogue to quality Internet resources in the health and life sciences.

610 Medicine

- *National Library of Medicine (http://www.nlm.nih.gov)*

  The National Library of Medicine's website includes news and links to other health and medicine resources.

620 Engineering

- *SearchIt Engineering (http://searchit.engineering.co.uk)*

  Database for learning and teaching materials in engineering. Free of charge.

- *Aerade (http://aerade.cranfield.ac.uk)*

  The Aerade portal provides access to key aerospace and defence information sources, including quality Internet sites, a special collection of military and defence resources, abstracts for engineering design data and methods, an interactive tutorial, and aerospace and defence news.

- *PORT National Maritime Museum (http://www.port .nmm.ac.uk)*

  Premier portal of high-quality maritime resources on the Internet, maintained by the National Maritime Museum. Appropriate resources are selected, evaluated and catalogued. Prominence is given to UK resources. Includes the:

- *Maritime Memorials (http://www.nmm.ac.uk/memorials/ index.cfm)*

  This recently launched memorial database contains records of over 4,000 church, cemetery and public memorials to seafarers and victims of maritime disasters.

650 Management and public relations

- *Altis (http://www.altis.ac.uk)*

  Altis is the guide to Internet resources in hospitality, leisure, sport and tourism. The site offers links to sites on such subjects as catering, hospitality studies, teaching and research, physical education, sports history, sports and leisure organisations, outdoor pursuits, leisure and tourism policy, planning and development, sustainable and ecotourism, tourism statistics, outdoor and countryside recreation.

A rather helpful feature is the Favourite Sites section. The people responsible for the content of Altis have asked people working within the hospitality, leisure, sport and tourism sector to recommend their favourite websites and describe how they found them useful in their learning, teaching and research. These recommendations have then been made available on Altis.

640 Home and family management

- *The Times Cook* (*http://www.jilldupleix.com*)
Jill Dupleix, the Times Cook, has her own beautifully designed website. Includes restaurant reviews from her husband and the recipe of the month.

700 Fine Arts and Recreation

700 Arts

- *ADAM gateway* (*http://adam.ac.uk*)
The resources on this gateway to art design, architecture and media information are carefully selected and catalogued by librarians for the benefit of the UK higher

education community. It will shortly be taken over by the new Arts and Creative Industries hub (ACI). Until the new hub is running, the ADAM gateway will still be a useable resource.

- *The Artists (http://www.the-artists.org)*

  Database containing the most important artists of the twentieth century. Free of charge.

- *Dover Bookshop (http://www.thedoverbookshop.com)*

  Bookshop specialising in copyright-free images and illustrations. Online ordering possible.

770 Photography

- *British Film Institute (http://www.bfi.org.uk)*

  This is an immense site, containing among other things a searchable online catalogue, OLIB Webview, which contains one of the world's largest collections of books on cinema and television. The collection of over 42,000 books covers all aspects of film and television internationally. As well as books about a particular film/person/subject, you can also use the catalogue to access the holdings of bibliographies, PhD theses, directories, yearbooks, annual reports, encyclopaedias, filmographies and published scripts.

  I think the most fascinating part of the British Film Institute's website is their list of the 100 best British films ever. It is a reflection on a full century of British film-making and an opinion poll of those involved in British film. The list is intended, and offered, as a starting-point for discussion.

I have used this list recently to stock up on our DVD collection in the library.

- *Librarians in the movies (http://www.byui.edu/Ricks/ employee/raishm/films/introduction.html)*

  Librarians in the movies: an annotated filmography, maintained by Martin Raish from the library at Brigham Young University in Idaho, is a great personal site. One can feel the personal interest and motivation. Raish's filmography is an attempt to find out whether the 'librarian stereotype' as portrayed in articles, letters, conversations, books and films is true. It lists over 400 Hollywood films that in some significant way include a library or a librarian.

- *Internet Movie Database (http://www.imdb.com)*

  I use this huge database when cataloguing DVD films and cannot be bothered to read the small type, or can't find the year the film was made on the DVD. Also very good if you want to stock up on a particular actor or director.

- *Movie Scripts (http://www.movie-page.com/movie_scripts .htm)*

  This is a fascinating collection of full-text film scripts (in Word or PDF), ranging from *The Abyss* to *Thelma & Louise*.

780 Music

- *Allmusicguide (http://www.allmusic.com)*

  Comprehensive music dictionary on most styles, written by music journalists. Free of charge.

790 Sports, games and entertainment

■ *Allsports (http://www.allsports.com)*

Comprehensive information on most sports. Free of charge.

800 Literature, Rhetoric and Criticism

■ *Eurodicautom (http://europa.eu.int/eurodicautom)*

European terminology database, translation into 12 languages. Free of charge.

■ *Bartleby (http://www.bartleby.com)*

Claims to be the pre-eminent Internet publisher of literature, reference and verse, providing students, researchers and the intellectually curious with unlimited access to books and information on the web, free of charge. Reference works include, among many others: *Columbia Encyclopaedia*, 6th edn, 2001; *The Encyclopaedia of World History*, 6th edn, 2001; *The Columbia Gazetteer of North America*, 2000 and *The World Fact Book 2001*.

In the reference section on religion and mythology, the King James version of the Bible is online; and in literary history and literature you will find the *Cambridge History of English and American Literature* (18 vols) and *The Oxford Shakespeare*, 1914. There is also *Henry Gray's Anatomy of the Human Body*, 1918, 20th edn, online in full text.

Other full-text works are available on this website from authors as diverse as Theodore Roosevelt, Jean Jacques Rousseau, Eugene O'Neill, Gertrude Stein and Walt Whitman, to name but a (very) few. The site also includes a weekly poem – when I checked the site for this book, it was Robert Frost's *The Road Not Taken.*

900 Geography and History

910 Geography and travel

■ *Mapblast (http://www.mapblast.com)*
World atlas with detailed town and street database. Free of charge.

■ *The World of Maps (http://www.maps.ethz.ch)*
Gateway for maps and mapping. Maps, spacial data, map collections, map archives, map curatorship and history, and links to catalogues of map holdings.

940 History of Europe

■ *Perseus Digital Library (http://www.perseus.tufts.edu)*
Perseus is an evolving digital library, engineering interactions through time, space and language. Their primary goal is to bring a wide range of source materials to a large audience. The Perseus Classics collection began as an integrated collection of materials – textual and visual – on the Archaic and Classical Greek world. Named after the Hellenic hero who explored the world to its most distant reaches, Perseus made it possible for specialists and non-specialists alike to move between traditionally distinct types of information, such as images and texts, and across traditionally distinct disciplines, such as classical

archaeology and philology. Building on the success of the tools and resources developed for Ancient Greek source materials, the project expanded into the Roman world, with additional art and archaeology materials as well as new collections of Latin texts and tools.

The collection contains extensive and diverse resources, including primary and secondary texts, site plans, digital images and maps. Art and archaeology catalogues document a wide range of objects: over 1,500 vases, over 1,800 sculptures and sculptural groups, over 1,200 coins, hundreds of buildings from nearly 100 sites and over 100 gems. Catalogue entries are linked to tens of thousands of images, many in high resolution, and have been produced in collaboration with many museums, institutions and scholars. Immense and comprehensive.

Notes

1. *http//www.oecd.org*
2. Alice Calaprice (ed.) (2002) *Dear Professor Einstein*. Prometheus Books.
3. *http//www.oclc.org/dewey/about*

7

Keeping up to date

Polonius: What do you read, my lord?
Hamlet: Words, words, words.

William Shakespeare, 1564–1616

It is a known fact that it will never be possible to make all existing information and the whole of human knowledge available in a digital format. Therefore, we are forced to use other search tools to get the information we are looking for. Even if we had mastered all search techniques, if we knew all available databases, if we were registered with all online services and if we were always on top of new developments, there will always be something new to learn, something unknown to explore – and perhaps we might realise that sometimes it is just as well that we do not know everything.

In this chapter, I would like to offer you a few suggestions on how you may be able to keep up with the rapid developments and the demands that are made in your job. Ultimately, being on top of things will give you the confidence and the knowledge to serve and support your customers to the best of your ability. Use the Internet as a working tool. It is there to help you with your job.

Strategies for keeping up to date

Use the Web to your advantage – make use of the resources on offer. There certainly has to be a willingness to embrace change. In my experience, the following strategies have helped me greatly in my job:

- personal networks;
- reading;
- daily practice;
- newsletters;
- library mailing lists and discussion groups;
- special interest groups;
- conferences and training;
- professional fora;
- job vacancies, recruiting and employment.

Personal networks

Never underestimate the power of personal networks! Keep those business cards and telephone numbers that are always exchanged at meetings and conferences, and put them in your organiser, be it paper or electronic. Do not throw them away, even if you have not used them in years. How many times, after a spring-cleaning session at my desk, have I regretted throwing a business card away when I could have used it two days later.

- *Public Library Networking Focus (http://www.ukoln.ac .uk/public)*

    The Public Library Networking Focus aims to contribute to strategic policy-making, awareness raising and developing activities in the area of public library networking and lifelong learning.

Reading

Read, read, read! Read everything concerning the Internet and search strategies that you can lay your hands on. Read the relevant sections in your newspaper, read the articles in the commuter newspapers like *Metro*, read lifestyle magazines, read the articles in the tabloid press – because this is what most people, including some of your customers, will read. It gives you an advantage to know what others read. Follow up this reading with the reading of professional articles so that you have the technical or scientific background. Or, as Sir Richard Steele (1672–1729) put it: 'Reading is to the mind what exercise is to the body.'

Daily practice

Use the Web daily. Play with it. Practise on it. I cannot stress this point enough. Even if you have a very busy day and do not know whether you are coming or going, take some time and 'exercise' on the Internet for a couple of minutes. Try something out. Perhaps you could try to formulate a search query and test it in various search engines and compare the results. Learn something new every day and use the things that you have learned. And another thing: do not be afraid of passing the things you have learned on to other people. In my experience 'it is not a good kind of power that one gets through knowledge', even if Francis Bacon and probably many others thought so and still do.

Newsletters

It is important to keep up-to-date with new developments and this is easy if other professionals make a brilliant job of collecting and disseminating worthwhile developments.

■ *The Internet Resources Newsletter (http://www.hw.ac.uk/libwww/irn/irn.html)*

The Internet Resources Newsletter, edited by Roddy MacLeod, Catherine Ure and Catherine Ferguson from the Heriot Watt University Library in Edinburgh, is a free monthly newsletter for academics, students, engineers and scientists. Subscribing is easy. Just leave your e-mail address on their website.

Library mailing lists and discussion groups

Professional discussion groups are a good means to share experiences, to enhance collaboration, to keep in touch with other professionals, to make new contacts and to keep up to date with advancements. You might consider subscribing to one or two carefully selected discussion lists. Before you subscribe, make sure that you read through some of the postings in order to get an idea of the style and level used in that particular list. Below follows a selection of some library discussion lists:

■ *LIS-LINK (http://www.jiscmail.ac.uk/lists/LIS-LINK.html)*

LIS-LINK is a general library and information science list for news and discussion. Items are discussed of general interest to library and information science professionals in higher education and research institutions in the UK and elsewhere.

- *IFLA-L (http://www.ifla.org/IIlists/ifla-l.htm)*

  IFLA-L is the mailing list of the International Federation of Library Associations. The electronic forum is intended to foster communications between IFLA members and the international library community.

- *JISCmail (http://www.jiscmail.ac.uk)*

  JISCmail is a mailing list service for higher and further education communities in the UK, enabling members to stay in touch and share information by e-mail or via the Web.

  The lists on JISCmail are free to the academic community and easy to use either via e-mail or web browser. JISCmail hosts thousands of lists on a huge variety of different subjects. The list below is a small extract:

  - LIB-DISASTER   Library disaster forum
  - LIBQUAL-UK   The UK LibQual+ Interest Group
  - LIBRARY-REVIEW   Review of the public library service in England and Wales
  - LIFELEARN   Lifelong learning mailing list
  - LIHNN   A list for health-related libraries within the north-west of England
  - LIP_SW   Libraries in Partnership South West
  - LIS-ACCESS   Library support to 'non-traditional' students

– LIS-ACQ	For anyone with an interest in acquisitions issues (non-serial)
– LIS-ARC	Academic Reference Centre
– LIS-BAILER	Information and/or Library Studies in the UK
– LIS-BIN LINC	Business Information Panel
– LIS-CAIRNS	Co-operative Academic Information Retrieval Network for Scotland
– LIS-CIGS	Cataloguing of electronic resources, etc.
– LIS-CILIP	Chartered Library and Information Professionals
– LIS-CILIP-REG	List for CILIP members working towards MCLIP status
– LIS-CONTIN-ED	Adult and Continuing Education Librarians
– LIS-CUMBRIA	LINC – Library Information Network Cumbria
– LIS-E-BOOKS	E-books in academic libraries mailing list
– LIS-E-JOURNALS	An informal open list set up by the UK Serials Group
– LIS-E-THESES	Electronic thesis issues among the academic community
– LIS-EDUC	Library services for education
– LIS-ELIB JISC	Electronic Libraries Programme
– LIS-ELIB-TECH	Technical issues relating to the eLib projects

- *Link list at the Zentral- und Landesbibliothek (http:// www.zlb.de/bibliothek/fachbereiche/infdienste/fremdspr/ englisch/index.html)*

A good collection of library mailing lists can be found on the site of the Zentral- und Landesbibliothek in Berlin.

Special interest groups

- *Aslib, The Association for Information Management (http://www.aslib.co.uk/sigs/index.html)*

A good way to network is to be a member of a special interest group. Aslib offers various groups and is open to all individuals. There is no need for your organisation to be an Aslib member. The following Aslib special interest groups are active:

- Biosciences Group
- Charitable Information Group
- Economics and Business Information Group
- Knowledge and Information Management Network
- IT & Communications
- Multimedia Group
- One Man Bands Group
- Social Sciences Information Group and Network
- Technical Translation Group
- European Business Opportunities Service.

There are also regional branches:

- Midlands Branch
- Northern Branch
- Scottish Branch.

The Membership Department has more information:

Tel: +(44) 020 7903 0000

Fax: +(44) 020 7903 0011

E-mail: *members@aslib.com*

- *University Science and Technology Librarians Group* (*http://www.leeds.ac.uk/library/ustlg*)

    Another example of an interest group is USTLG, the University Science and Technology Librarians Group, an informal group which tries to meet two or three times a year to discuss any topics of interest to members. They say it is a very useful way to keep in touch and to get to know colleagues in other libraries.

Conferences and training

- *CILIP* (*http://www.cilip.org.uk*)

    CILIP (the Chartered Institute of Library and Information Professionals) offers a varied training and development programme. Their courses include:

    - Financial and performance management
    - Internet skills
    - Interpersonal skills
    - Teaching, learning and development
    - Management skills
    - Marketing and fundraising
    - Professional and technical skills.

- *BUBL* (*http://www.bubl.ac.uk/news/events*)

    Information on library and information science conferences, workshops, meetings and courses can be found on BUBL.

■ *Aslib Training (http://www.aslib.co.uk/training/index.html)*

Aslib Training provides training in the form of public courses, on-site training, conferences and distance learning. Their programme includes:

   – Business and official information sources
   – General management and communication skills
   – Knowledge management
   – Managing Internet sites.

Professional fora

A good way to keep abreast of developments and in touch with your peers is to subscribe to a forum. A professional forum has the advantage that it is usually moderated and only used by other professionals.

■ *Managing Information (http://www.managinginformation .com)*

The discussion board on the website of *Managing Information* is moderated by the editor, and all illegal or offensive messages will be deleted. It also clearly states that participants are asked to comply with UK and international copyright law.

Job vacancies, recruiting and employment

If you decide to change your job, many job offers and vacancies may be found on the Internet.

■ *Free Pint (http://www.freepint.com/jobs)*

Free Pint is a global network of over 60,000 information researchers. They offer, among other things, a weekly e-mail notification of the newest jobs available in the industry. As the name suggests, free of charge.

- *Glen Recruitment (http://www.glenrecruitment.co.uk)*

  Independent employment agency specialising in the recruitment of information specialists, knowledge professionals, business analysts, researchers, librarians and online support staff.

- *BUBL (http://www.bubl.ac.uk/news/jobs)*

  BUBL information service also offers job vacancies.

- *Aslib (http://www.aslib.co.uk/recruit/sys/jobs_main.php)*

  Aslib professional recruitment specialises in recruiting and supplying permanent and temporary staff. Searchable database.

Your own favourite websites

A good way to keep your knowledge up to date is to maintain your own personal list of favourites on your web browser. You may look at it as your very own personal reference desk. Take your time to compile a list and see whether the links still work once a month, or once every three months – as long as you do it on a regular basis. It would be logical to use the same categories as with your public list though the contents would be different. You would want to add links that you use in your daily work. You would certainly need links to the following:

- reference services;

- translation aids;

- news;

- time and weather;

- transport and travel information;

- libraries and literature.

Below is what a favourites list might look like (using the above category list) for a librarian working in a small community library.

Reference services

- *Cambridge Dictionaries Online (http://dictionary .cambridge.org)*

  A search for 'library' in the *Cambridge International Dictionary of English* found the entries listed below:

  – library;
  – lending library;
  – mobile library;
  – reference library.

  The Cambridge International Dictionary of English is a very handy tool indeed.

- *Your Dictionary (http://www.yourdictionary.com/)*

  Comprehensive index of online dictionaries in more than 200 different languages. Includes an index of online grammars. Free of charge.

- *Libraryspot (http://www.libraryspot.com)*

  Library and reference resources, including dictionaries, encyclopaedias, newspapers, maps and quotations.

- *Librarians' Index to the Internet (http://www.lii.org)*

  Claims to be a well-organised point of access for reliable, trustworthy, librarian-selected Internet resources. The index is searchable, annotated and contains more than 10,000 Internet resources selected and evaluated by librarians for their usefulness to users of public libraries.

  Also has a good current awareness service, the 'New This Week Mailing List'. The list sent at the beginning of April 2003 contained resources on the Iraq war and information related to SARS, the Severe Acute Respiratory Syndrome.

Statistical data has become, over the past couple of years, very widely available on the Internet. Most international, national and regional statistical organisations and data sources are now available online. However, not all services are free of charge.

- *CIA World Factbook (http://www.cia.gov/cia/publications/factbook)*

  Who has not heard of the CIA World Factbook? It is a reliable and, mostly, up-to-date source of statistical information on countries and their people and economy.

- *World Health Organisation (http://www.who.int)*

  Statistical health data. Search under 'Health Topics' for 'Statistics of Epidemiology'.

- *United Nations Statistics Division (http://unstats.un.org/ unsd/default.htm)*

  Compilation from many international sources – including the Statistical Yearbook – and yearbooks in specialised fields of statistics. Unrestricted free access to selected global datasets, such as the Millennium Indicators Database, which presents 48 social and economic indicators and related series by country and year since 1985. Further data only by subscription.

Translation aids

- *Link to dictionaries (http://math-www.uni-paderborn.de/ HTML/Dictionaries.html)*

  A comprehensive site of dictionaries of many languages and terms, maintained by the Universities of Paderborn in Germany.

- *The New Geordie Dictionary (http://www.geordiepride .demon.co.uk/dictionary.htm)*

  The New Geordie Dictionary, presented by the Concise Oxford Dictionary.

News

Many search engines and portals offer news services. Yahoo! and Google, among others, offer a dedicated page with links to over 4,000 news stories all over the world, continually updated. The big national newspapers and television stations usually offer good online news services.

- *The Daily Telegraph (http://www.telegraph.co.uk)*

  The Daily Telegraph has news stories on the front page, including breaking news. Registration gives access to deeper levels of *telegraph.co.uk* content. Free of charge.

- *The Times (http://www.timesonline.co.uk)*

  The Times also offers breaking news. Recently, a new policy was introduced to overseas readers: an annual subscription fee of £39.99 for overseas readers of the newspaper editions. Overseas readers are asked to pay the subscription fee after logging in or registering as a new user.

- *BBC (http://www.bbc.co.uk)*

  The online version of the BBC is an immense, very well-made site. It is possible to access local information by entering one's postcode or town name. The BBC site also has a good news ticker.

- *Newspapers US and Worldwide (http://www.onlinenews papers.com)*

  Newspapers US and Worldwide offers a comprehensive listing of world newspapers, with a focus on American newspapers.

- *Foreign language news and newspapers (http://libraries .mit.edu/guides/types/flnews)*

  Foreign language news and newspapers, electronic journals, newspapers and magazines are available from the Massachusetts Institute of Technology site *MIT Libraries*. The well-maintained site contains a link collection to electronic journals, newspapers and magazines in Chinese, French, German, Italian, Japanese, Portuguese, Russian and Spanish. As it is part of the Institute, it contains no ads, which is a great plus.

- *The World Press (http://www.theworldpress.com)*

The World Press homepage offers a, not quite, comprehensive listing of world newspapers, listed by country.

- *Newspapers on the Net (http://www.onlinenewspapers.com)*

Newspapers on the Net lists over 10,000 newspapers from around the world, searchable by country and then by publication. Very comprehensive.

- *English-edition daily newspapers (personal homepage) (http://www.inkdrop.net/dave/news.html)*

This personal homepage links to English-edition dailies. Nearly all of these are English-edition daily newspapers, with an emphasis on the Middle East and Asia. They are included because they have interesting editorials and essays, and many have links to other good news sources. This page is a good example of how personal homepages can be very good and comprehensive.

Time and weather

- *Greenwich Mean Time (http://greenwichmeantime.com)*

If you were to be asked: 'What time is it anywhere in the world?', then the official site of Greenwich is the place to go. It offers the global time zones, listed country by country. The site also has a very comprehensive and interesting link list.

■ *Meteorological Office (http://www.metoffice.com)*

Among other data and information there is a rainfall animation that shows rainfall radar images at hourly intervals. There is also satellite imagery to see the weather from space. Links to other weather resources.

Transport and travel information

It might be a good idea to have further travel information available, complementary to the books on offer on the library shelves. Here you might want to concentrate on the transport available in your region and the most important national companies along with some good travel and holiday gateways. Your list may then look something like this:

■ *Scotrail (http://www.scotrail.co.uk)*

Scotland's national railway.

■ *Nationalrail (http://www.nationalrail.co.uk)*

Gateway to Britain's national rail network.

■ *Citylink (http://www.citylink.co.uk)*

Scotland's leading provider of Express Coach services. Online timetable and comprehensive link list to all major tourist and travel sites within the UK.

■ *Traveline (http://www.traveline.org.uk)*

Travel gateway. For planning any public transport journeys by bus, coach or train within Scotland and from Scotland to main points in the UK.

Libraries and literature

■ *British Library (http://www.bl.uk)*

In its own words, the British Library gives access to 'the world's knowledge'.

■ *Library of Congress (http://www.loc.gov)*

Largest library in the world, with more than 120 million items. The collections (some of it viewable online) include more than 18 million books, 2.5 million recordings, 12 million photographs, 4.5 million maps and 54 million manuscripts. Also links to 'Thomas', which includes among other things the schedule of the American Senate.

■ *Literature Awards (http://www.literature-awards.com)*

A listing of over 170 literature awards for fiction, non-fiction, biography, autobiography, children's literature, poetry, science fiction, horror, drama, mystery and fantasy.

■ *Pulitzer Prize (http://www.pulitzer.org)*

The homepage of the famous literary award includes a searchable list of prize winners, a history of the prize, guidelines and entry forms, and contact information.

In their Frequently Asked Questions list is the interesting question of how 'Pulitzer' is pronounced! (The correct pronunciation is 'PULL it sir'.)

■ *Contemporary Writers in the UK (http://www .contemporarywriters.com)*

This unique, searchable database contains up-to-date profiles of some of the UK and Commonwealth's most important living writers – biographies, bibliographies, critical reviews, prizes and photographs. Searchable by author, genre, nationality, gender, publisher, book title, date of publication and prize name and date. The views expressed are those of the contributors and do not necessarily represent those of the British Council or Book Trust. Beautifully made homepage.

- *Information about the book world (http://www.book trust.org.uk)*

  If you want to find out about books published in the UK and US since 1900, this is the page to visit. It also offers information on new and forthcoming books, publishers and prizes. Newsletter, listings for literary magazines, events and a series of fact sheets are also available.

- *London Review of Books (http://www.lrb.co.uk)*

  The *London Review of Books* was founded in 1979, during the year-long lock-out at *The Times*. For the first six months, the LRB appeared as an insert in the *New York Review of Books*. In May 1980, the *London Review of Books* jumped out of the parental pouch and became a fully independent literary paper. It has been published twice a month ever since. The *London Review of Books* has been dedicated to carrying on the tradition of the English essay. In this respect, it is not very different from one of the great nineteenth-century periodicals. It gives its contributors the space and freedom to develop their ideas at length and in depth.

- *New York Review of Books (http://www.nybooks.com/about)*

  With a national circulation of over 115,000, the *New York Review of Books* has established itself, in *Esquire*'s words, as 'the premier literary-intellectual magazine in the English language'. The *New York Review* began its life during the New York publishing strike of 1963, and now a newsletter and selected articles from the current issue are readable online free of charge.

- *Whitbread Book Awards (http://www.whitbread-book awards.co.uk)*

  The Whitbread is one of the longest-running and most prestigious book awards in the UK. Since its launch in 1971, its structure has evolved, but it has never deviated from its original ethos of identifying and celebrating some of the most enjoyable books published in the UK. There are six awards in total – five category awards (Novel, First Novel, Biography, Poetry and Children's) and, from these, one overall winner – the Whitbread Book of the Year.

- *Banned Books Online (http://onlinebooks.library .upenn.edu)*

  This is an extensive directory of links to online texts that have been the object of censorship or censorship attempts. The books featured here range from *Ulysses* to *Little Red Riding Hood*. The page claims to be a work in progress, and more works may be added over time. They ask readers to inform them of any new material that can be included there. Note that the listings are meant to be representative rather than exhaustive.

Tutorials

A good way to keep ahead of things is to dedicate some time regularly to build on your existing knowledge. A way to do this is to visit the many web tutorials on offer. They allow you to work in your own time at your own pace – no one is monitoring you!

- *The RDN Virtual Training Suite (http://www.vts.rdn.ac.uk)*

  The Virtual Training Suite, maintained by the Resource Discovery Network, is a set of online tutorials designed to help students, lecturers and researchers improve their Internet information literacy and IT skills.

- *Learn the Net (http://www.learnthenet.com)*

  Another brilliant site, Learn the Net offers many helpful chapters. They have also got some fun stuff, like 'Get an astronaut's view of the world'. Of more professional interest are their Today's Top Tech Stories with the latest news. You can enrol in interactive classes such as 'Understanding the World Wide Web', 'Communicate Effectively with E-Mail' or 'Protect Yourself Online'. There is also a rather wonderful animated show explaining how encryption works. In addition, an Internet quiz allows you to test your Internet IQ and there is even an Internet crossword.

8

Perfect customer service

Faultily faultless, icily regular, splendidly null,
Dead perfection, no more.

Alfred, Lord Tennyson, 1809–92

We are not responsible for the content of a website. We do not have to be angry, arrogant or helpless about it. But we have a responsibility and a fundamental duty as librarians or information workers to help people find what they want, and perhaps even make them happy in the process. It is our duty as people who work in the service industry – and a library belongs to that category.

It is very important for the image of a library for staff to display the correct conduct when handling customer enquiries. How the service of the library is perceived by its customers has much to do with how we treat the library customer.

A library plays an important part in the education of people and one of the main purposes of a public library is to give people access to literature and information. People need help to find, evaluate and use information effectively. Libraries help people to develop and maintain reading skills, and literacy and numeracy facilitate participation in the wider context of lifelong learning and contribute to the social integration of individuals. According to Sheila Corrall, President of CILIP (the Chartered Institute of

Library and Information Professionals), information skills are critical to the achievement of the social, educational, professional and business goals of our communities. She says that information skills are needed:

- to bridge the 'digital divide';
- to enable independent learning;
- to support evidence-based decisions;
- to counter information overload;
- to retrieve information from the 'invisible web';
- to manage knowledge and intellectual capital.

We librarians should be aware that offering good service to customers is one of the main aspects of our job – which is to support readers in their search for information and literature as far as possible. All the work that is done in the 'back office', such as accession, cataloguing, etc. is only done for the benefit of the customer and not as a means in itself or because it is fun to catalogue books. Contact between library customers and librarians mainly happens at the reference and lending desks. Librarians who deal with customers on a daily or regular basis should have the following qualities well-developed:

- We should always strive to be friendly, patient, courteous, polite and considerate.
- We should be approachable and easy to make contact with.
- We should have a readiness and willingness to help customers and to provide good service.
- We should be well-balanced, calm and composed.

- We should be open-minded, sociable and take pleasure in handling literature enquiries.

A librarian must be able to connect with the customer and explain the library, its stock and lending conditions in a language that the customer understands. A new library customer has no way of knowing what key words, notations, etc. mean. We have to understand and know our customers. We have to listen to our customers. We have to be able to translate 'our' library language into ordinary language. We should never forget that it is we who are the specialists, not our customers, in the library world.

In order to offer the best service and correct conduct towards our customers, it is a prerequisite that we judge ourselves and our profession to the highest standards. This means that we must be competent and possess the required skills and knowledge. As librarians, we fulfil a – sometimes small, sometimes large – cultural and social duty. Therefore librarians should see themselves as partners of the library user and should deal with the customer in a spirit of friendly cooperation.

Index of Internet addresses

For easy reference all Internet resources mentioned in this book are listed below in alphabetical order.

Bartleby	*http://www.bartleby.com*
BBC	*http://www.bbc.co.uk*
Biology Browser	*http://www.biologybrowser.org*
BIOME Health and Life Sciences hub	*http://biome.ac.uk*
Book Trust, Information about the book world	*http://www.booktrust.org.uk*
BrightPlanet	*http://www.brightplanet.com*
British Film Institute	*http://www.bfi.org.uk*
British Library	*http://ww.bl.uk*
BUBL	*http://www.bubl.ac.uk*
Cambridge Online Dictionary	*http://dictionary.cambridge.org*
Cars.com	*http://www.cars.com*
CD Now	*http://www.cdnow.com*
Checkdomain	*http://www.checkdomain.com*
Chemdex	*http://www.chemdex.org*
Chemfinder	*http://www.chemfinder.com*
CIA World Factbook	*http://www.cia.gov/cia/ publications/factbook*
CILIP (Chartered Institute of Library and Information Professionals)	*http://www.cilip.org.uk*
Citylink	*http://www.citylink.co.uk*
Collection of library mailing lists	*http://www.zlb.de/bibliothek/ fachbereiche/infdienste/fremdspr/ englisch/index.html*
Complete Planet	*http://www.completeplanet.com*
Contemporary Writers in the UK	*http://www.contemporary writers.com*
Cornell Computer Science Technical Report Collection	*http://cs-tr.cs.cornell.edu*
Daily Telegraph	*http://www.telegraph.co.uk*
Direct Search	*http://www.freepint.com/gary/ direct.htm*
Directories of Mathematics Journals	*http://www.shef.ac.uk/library/ elecjnls/ejmaths.html*
Dogpile	*http://www.dogpile.com*
Dover Bookshop	*http://www.thedoverbookshop.com*
Easysearcher	*http://www.easysearcher.com*

Lacnic Regional Latin-American and Caribbean ID address registry	*http://lacnic.net*
Lawlinks	*http://www.ukc.ac.uk/library/ lawlinks/default.htm*
Learn the Net	*http://www.learnthenet.com*
LexisNexis	*http://www.lexisnexis.com*
Librarians in the Movies	*http://www.byui.edu/ricks/ employee/raishm/films/ introduction.html*
Librarians' Index to the Internet	*http://www.lii.org*
Library of Congress	*http://www.loc.gov*
Libraryspot	*http://www.libraryspot.com*
Lindley Library	*http://www.rhs.org.uk/libraries _london.asp*
Link to dictionaries	*http://math-www.uni-paderborn.de/ HTML/Dictionaries.html*
LIS-LINK	*http://www.jiscmail.ac.uk/lists/ LIS-LINK.html*
Liszt	*http://www.liszt.com*
Literature Awards	*http://www.literature-awards.com*
Liza Dalby	*http://www.lizadalby.com*
London Review of Books	*http://www.lrb.co.uk/*
Looksmart	*http://www.looksmart.com*
Lycos	*http://www.lycos.com*
Managing Information	*http://www.managing information.com*
Mapblast	*http://www.mapblast.com*
Maritime Memorials	*http://www.nmm.ac.uk/memorials/ index.cfm*
Mathforum	*http://www.mathforum.org*
Metacrawler	*http://www.metacrawler.com*
Metaspy	*http://www.metaspy.com*
Meteorological Office	*http://www.metoffice.com*
Microsoft	*http://www.microsoft.com*
Microsoft Network Search	*http://search.msn.com*
Mimas Database	*http://dois.mimas.ac.uk*
Movie Scipts	*http://www.movie-page.com/ movie_scripts.htm*

Scibase	*http://www.thescientificworld.com*
Scotrail	*http://www.scotrail.co.uk*
Search Engine Watch	*http://www.searchenginewatch.com/ links/major.html*
Searchit Engineering	*http://searchit.engineering.co.uk*
Shell Company	*http://www.shell.co.uk*
SOSIG (Social Science, Business and Law Hub)	*http://www.sosig.ac.uk*
SPIRES HEP Literature Database	*http://www.slac.stanford.edu/ spires/hep*
Stanford Encyclopedia of Philosophy	*http://plato.stanford.edu*
Subject Directory of Search Engines	*http://library.albany.edu/internet/ choose.html*
Switch Swiss Education and Research Network	*http://www.switch.ch*
Tale of Murasaki, Liza Dalby	*http://www.taleofmurasaki.com*
Techtarget	*http://whatis.techtarget.com*
Teoma	*http://www.teoma.com*
The Artists	*http://www.the-artists.org*
The Daily Telegraph	*http://www.telegraph.co.uk*
The Humbul Humanities Hub	*http://www.humbul.ac.uk*
The NASA Astrophysics data system	*http://adswww.harvard.edu*
The New Geordie Dictionary	*http://www.geordiepride.demon .co.uk/dictionary.htm*
The Times	*http://www.timesonline.co.uk*
The Times Cook	*http://www.jilldupleix.com*
The World of Maps	*http://www.maps.ethz.ch*
The World Press	*http://www.theworldpress.com*
Traveline	*http://www.traveline.org.uk*
United Nations Statistics Division	*http://unstats.un.org/unsd/ default.htm*
University of St Andrews	*http://www-gap.dcs-st-and.ac.uk/~ history/Mathematicians/Nash .html*
University, Science and Technology Librarians Group	*http://www.leeds.ac.uk/library/ustlg*
Virtual Training Suite	*http://www.vts.rdn.ac.uk/*

Wayback Machine	*http://www.archive.org*
Webcrawler	*http://www.webcrawler.com*
Whitbread Book Awards	*http://www.whitbread-bookawards .co.uk*
WHO World Health Organisation	*http://www.who.int*
Wisenut	*http://www.wisenut.com*
World of Biography – Physicists	*http://scienceworld.wolfram.com/ biography/topics/physicists.html*
Xrefer	*http://www.xrefer.com*
Yahoo!	*http://www.yahoo.com*
Your Dictionary	*http://www.yourdictionary.com/*
ZDNet	*http://www.zdnet.com*

Index

Printed in the United Kingdom
by Lightning Source UK Ltd.
111469UKS00001B/58